Cuisine Après Dentist

Cuisine Après Dentist

JIM MORAN

Rutledge Books, Inc.   Danbury, CT

Rutledge Books, Inc.
107 Mill Plain Road, Danbury, CT 06811
1-800-278-8533
www.rutledgebooks.com

Manufactured in the United States of America

Cataloging in Publication Data
Moran, Jim
  Cuisine Après Dentist

  ISBN: 1-58244-113-8

  1. Cookbook. 2. Eating for Healthy Teeth.

Library of Congress Catalog Card Number: 00-111427

Table
of
Contents

TO HAVE PERFECT TEETH,
CAREFULLY SELECT YOUR PARENTS,
OTHERWISE BRUSH
AND FLOSS LIKE THE REST OF US.

ACKNOWLEDGMENTS

*N*o human experience is entirely the result of the actions of one man or one woman. The manuscript for this book was influenced by many talented people. I am particularly indebted to the late Doctor Mark D. Elliott, D.M.D., orthodontist and distinguished member of the American Dental Association, whose gentle humor and wide knowledge have been both a guide and an inspiration. Doctors Philip F.M. Gilley Jr., D.D.S., Arthur P. Wein, D.D.S., Denise A. Mills, D.D.S., as well as others have made helpful and significant contributions.

Numerous chefs, some famous and some just good cooks, have given counsel, for example, Vincent Guerithault of Phoenix, Bill Nelson, San Francisco, Bob Holmes, Fitchburg, Massachusetts, Claire Tousignant, Tilton, New Hampshire, Robert Rosales, Scottsdale, and members of the Scottsdale Culinary Institute. Many restaurant operators as well as bed-and-breakfast owners have shared their recipes and ideas for feeding the tooth impaired. I am also indebted to a multitude of dental patients who have "down loaded" their tired gums in the hopes of finding sustenance.

For the countless hours of attentive effort that occur between the spawning of an idea and the completion of a manuscript, I acknowledge the unfailing support of my wife Marti, the computer expertise of my son Mark, the suggestions of Pat Kite of *Writer's Digest,* the editorial assistance of Elizabeth Watson, chief librarian of the Fitchburg, Massachusetts, Public Library and the readings of the drafts by daughter-in-law, Barbara Smith Moran.

Jim Moran
Leominster, Massachusetts, September 25, 1999

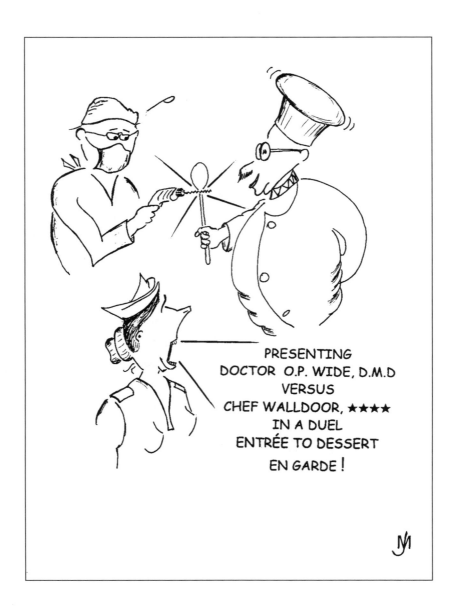

INTRODUCTION TO EATING AFTER DENTISTRY

*O*n an average day, more than two million persons are stewing in a waiting room marked *THE DENTIST IS IN*. Many of these people are asking themselves, "What am I going to have for dinner besides two aspirin and a milk toast sandwich?" This book is a whimsical guide to food preparation when you are undergoing molar maintenance. It can also point the way to better eating when your gums aren't the slightest bit interested in food.

We have asked cooks from around the world, "What do you eat when you have a toothache?" From 102 responses we have selected and refined over 60 tempting dishes for the tooth weary. Each recipe requires precious little chewing ability and has been served up with tasty stories that have been peppered with humor and salted with history.

Quite a few of these recipes can be prepared quickly with common ingredients. There are other suggestions which require more time and hands-on participation. You are urged to take the time to smell the aroma and indulge in some of the deep breathing, kitchen, therapeutic exercises. Therapeutic? Yes! When you're busy chopping onions you can't be wringing your hands.

An Asian philosopher once said that a picture is worth a thousand words. For every thousand or so words that you chew through, you will be rewarded with a cartoon that shows you how some of us act when we are in dental distress. You may even find one that describes how you feel when munching is a pain.

If you are among the rare breed who say, "I never have a toothache—going to the dentist is one of my recreational activities," you will be interested to know how the rest of us eat to live. You may also learn to love our Look-Ma-No-Teeth, Beef Burgundy Aspic, Apple-Onion Soup, Soft Sandwiches, Smashed Potatoes, and 57 other varieties of Easy-On-The-Teeth "goodies."

**IF YOU MUST GNASH YOUR TEETH
IT IS BETTER TO GNASH ON A
FULL STOMACH.**

List Of Illustrations

List Of Illustrations

Chapter 1

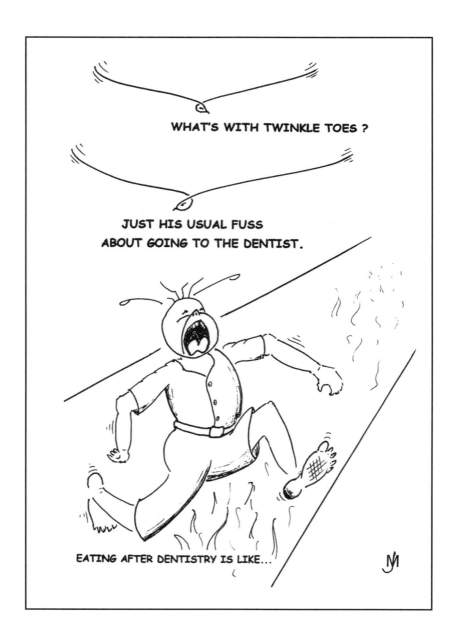

Filling A Tummy After Filling A Tooth

Eating after dentistry is sometimes like crossing a hot asphalt road in your bare feet; it only hurts while you're doing it.

A practical therapist once said, "You have three choices."

(1) Make it perfectly clear to everyone within vocal range that since you are having such a bad time it is only fair that they should suffer along with you.

(2) Go off and sulk by yourself. Above all, don't eat. This will elicit a few more crumbs of pity unless you run into some tough-love individual who insists, "You gotta eat something, even if it's chicken soup."

(3) Take a page from the diary of the wise mother who pondered what to tell her child when the going got to hurting. Timeless instincts supplied her with a philosophy that has produced survivors in this race of humans. She said simply, "This too will pass."

You can join the living circle of survivors by saying out loud, very loudly, "It will pass." Then, with the help of a doctor-recommended sedative, go fool around with some nourishment.

IT IS BETTER TO LIGHT A STOVE
THAN CURSE THE DARKNESS

Fantasize a fish or fowl that was once so tempting but has now retreated into no-no land. Is it possible to change such food into a satisfying morsel in your tooth impaired condition?

I remember one painful visit to the dentist when I had visions of a crab salad sandwich that I once enjoyed at a deli on Flatbush Avenue in Brooklyn. What made this a special "hero" was the blending of tender crabmeat, tomato, and sauces with aromatic dill and mustard and pepper, and thick crusty slabs of very, very rye bread. The thought of trying to bite into such a mouthful created a love-hate emotion not unlike French kissing a beautiful soul mate and waking up to find that it was the dog licking your face. If you can get the dog off of your face try the following recipe.

CRAB SALAD ON RYE
FOR
THE TOOTH WEARY

FOR 2 SERVINGS YOU NEED:

1 (10 3/4 oz.) can condensed TOMATO SOUP
1 (6 oz.) can CRAB MEAT
1 cup WATER, MILK, or HALF & HALF (Your choice)
1 teaspoon chopped DILL WEED
1/2 teaspoon DRY MUSTARD
1 teaspoon chopped PARSLEY
2 slices RYE BREAD
PEPPER & SALT to taste.

Remove the crust from the rye bread and place one piece in the bottom of each soup bowl. Heat and stir all of the other ingredients (except the parsley) in a medium size saucepan (about 6 minutes). If milk or cream was chosen, do NOT allow the mixture to boil. Pour the hot tomato crab over the rye bread. Add a bit of pepper and salt according to your taste, and drop the chopped parsley on the top. Let the warm liquid soften the tender bread, and think warm thoughts of tasty food and a better tomorrow, a tomorrow when this too will pass.

A can of tuna or salmon may be substituted for the crab meat.

There are a passel (see chapter 18 for complete exposé of words like *PASSEL, DASH, DOLLOP, SMIDGEN* and other cooking jargon) of ways to reduce chewing requirements and still preserve a semblance of sensuous biting satisfaction. Consider, for example, the social as well as the physical side of a procedure known as dunking. In a few Victorian sectors of our society, dunking has been "Emily Posted" as taboo. Many of us delight in the day when all closet dunkers will be able to come into an open dining room. With public dunking allowed, the dunker will be able to bring to the forefront the eater's participation in the food preparation process. A true dunker is one who is able to develop a style to fit their personal teething demands. They can adjust the time of dunk, allowing just enough crunchiness to satisfy their appetite while the tooth-nerve fairy is looking the other way. There is actually a movement brewing in some coffee bars to award a prize of two bagels to the Slam Dunker of the week. This is an honor reserved for a very few special achievers outside the basketball court.

I sat one morning in a small German Coffee House in Berlin. The locals called it Kaffee Haus Kurfurstendamm or simply Kaffee Ku'damm. I had enjoyed the good "damm" coffee, or as the Americans say, the damn good coffee. The pungent odor of fresh baked bread blended with the smell of crushed coffee beans to create a special dunker's Shangri-la. This particular morning, one of the regular signs on the counter had been altered. The numeral 9 in the 9-grain bread had a slash line through it and a bold number 10 had been added. When Hans, the baker-owner, came by my booth to spread philosophy and more coffee, I couldn't resist the question: "What's the tenth grain, or for that matter, what are the other nine?"

"It's the variety of the fibers," he replied in an accent that spoke Bavarian. "If you use many grains, and if you use all of the grain parts you get the good stuff. If you want to live to be a hundred and still have good teeth, you should eat my 10-grain bread. Start with wheat, add rye, barley, and oat flour. Then put in a little sunflower, sesame, and soy. Toss in a little corn and lentils."

· I made him repeat the list so that I could be sure that I had counted only nine. "Whoa," I said in a scurrilous tone, "What happened to the tenth?"

"The tenth, my bread dunking friend, is a grain of common sense. I have always tried to add this ingredient to my baking. Until now, I never thought about advertising it. Yesterday, I went over to Lietzenburger Square to see what the competition was doing. They had just changed their bread from 6 grain to 9 grain."

JUST IGNORE YOUR TEETH AND
THEY WILL GO AWAY.

Chapter 2

Making The Most Of Precious
After-Dentist Time

A very smart homemaker once said, "Never shop for food with an empty stomach." When you are hungry, your drooling glands team up with your impulse genie. Two weeks later, as you look at three cans of Senegalese snails on your pantry shelf, you will say, "I must have been out of my gourd to buy this stuff."

There is no better time to shop wisely than after you have eaten a full meal, or after a full-blown dental session.

The full benefit to shopping après dentist can be realized as you approach the check out counter. Instead of becoming upset with the fourth person ahead of you (the one who has reached the register and is insisting that their invalid coupons are not really invalid) simply engage the person directly ahead of you in conversation. Relate to them how fortunate they are to escape the agony that you are experiencing from your full-filled tooth. If you play your role right, and who among us is not a tiny bit of a stage player (some tinier than others), you could earn, "You poor thing, why don't you move up ahead of . . . Here! Move aside, let the tooth-handicap through."

See! You can turn your impediment into a plus. **CAUTION:** Do not repeat this same procedure at the same supermarket within the same thirty days.

You have just seated yourself at dinner and the phone rings with a talky telemarketer telling you about the merits of Megapane storm windows. The appropriate response is, "Sorry I have just returned from the dentist and I don't feel like discussing my stormy windows." All qualified, phone marketing personnel have been trained to say: "I am so sorry to hear of this misfortune, when may I call you?" With a little practice you can rattle off, "On February 30th." Believe me, if you keep after this tooth thing you can make a real career out of it.

JUST THINK OF ALL THE OPPORTUNITIES FOR SPREADING THIS PROBLEM AROUND.

CAN BE SUBSTITUTED FOR A HEADACHE IN A NUMBER OF MARITAL SITUATIONS.

CAN BE USED TO TURN DOWN A DINNER INVITATION FROM THE HOST OR HOSTESS WHO INSISTS ON SHOWING ENDLESS HOME VIDEOS.

After you become tired of these self-pity, self-destructive habits including the expression most heard on shrink couches, "Why does it always happen to me? Why, for God's sake, at this crucial time in my life?" Try, just try, to concentrate on a dish of food that you have always been going to make but have never taken the time to properly prepare.

There is a story about an octogenarian who loved a Waldorf salad but her teeth had difficulties with the walnuts which were part of the original recipe. Here is what she did:

A WALDORF SALAD
FOR
A TOUCHY TOOTH

FOR EACH TWO PEOPLE

YOU NEED:

2 tart APPLES, like Macintosh, Cortland, or Wine Sap
2 medium stalks CELERY
10 or 12 seedless GRAPES
4 tablespoons ORANGE or CRANBERRY JUICE
4 tablespoons MAYONNAISE
In place of the chopped walnuts that Oscar at the Waldorf used:
1/2 teaspoon ground CINNAMON
1/4 teaspoon ground NUTMEG

*D*ice the peeled apples, the celery, and grapes into tiny cubes. In a mixing bowl add the fruit juice, mayo, and spices to the diced ingredients and thoroughly mix with a fork.

Serving this salad on a leafy bit of lettuce makes it look enticing. If your teeth don't "do lettuce" enjoy the "Waldorf" and feed the lettuce to your pet rabbit.

There was a fellow who not only had a tooth problem but he had maturing eyesight. He had reached that time in life which occurs for many people when someone asks, "You mean to tell me you're actually 49 years old?" It is that time in life when vision can no longer be corrected with a simple, single, optical lens. His eye doctor measured him for a set of bifocals. His vanity measured him for a role in a Shakespearean tragedy. "Bifocals," he moaned. "Oh Lord, I'm an old man." But his wise optometrist saved his day. Knowing that his patient was into the latest in TV and computers, he said to the short-sighted fellow, "You're not wearing bifocals. You are using the split screen mode."

> **AS THE PHOTOGRAPHER SAID,**
> **"FOCUS FROM A NEW DIRECTION AND YOU**
> **WILL OFTEN IMPROVE YOUR PICTURE."**
>
>

Chapter 3

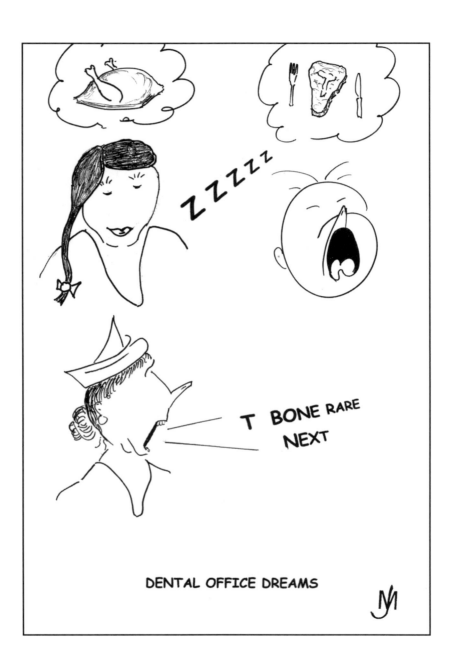

DENTAL OFFICE DREAMS

The Dentist's Chair Is Looking More Like A Psychiatrist's Couch

There was a time when the makers of barber chairs also made chairs for dental patients. Some dentists were perfectly happy with the tough-cushioned, masculine, barber seating arrangement but there were a few innovators who were seeking ways to improve the accuracy of the sign out front, *PAINLESS DENTISTRY*. The idea of getting patients to relax, like they were reclining on a chaise lounge in Palm Beach, occurred to several members of the American Dental Association. They took a leaf from the journals of Sigmund Freud who taught that complex ideas, like sex and pain, could best be handled while lying down. The modern dental couch, you might say, was conceived.

Some dental patients have suggested that the present-day waiting room be equipped with dental couches. Here, the patient could sleep and dream, or stew and drool, while waiting their turn to join that favorite part of civilization, the part that lives to eat.

Historians differ on the origins of the psychiatric, dental couch. Some suggest that the dental divan can be traced to the Emperor

Claudius in Rome. Claude always took his food (grapes) and his drink (fermented grapes) on a padded davenport. If he got a tooth or tummy ache he just lay there until the medics arrived. In his laid back condition he was easily accessible for either tooth pulling or tummy degassing.

What better way to spend after dentist time than by ravishing a Roman Ratatouille while resting on your sofa. The ratatouille is a Mediterranean version of vegetables prepared with a no-cholesterol oil. Food historians have said that ratatouille on a recliner enabled early residents of the Isle of Capri to live longer than their teeth. Today, with regular visits to your dentist, proper nourishment, and a daily walk, your teeth could outlive you.

Ratatouille is a widely accepted way of disguising zucchini and eggplant. In preparation you have a full choice of including, or omitting, any vegetable to match your desires. As any loyal member of the Sons of Italy, and some of the daughters, will tell you: "It's sort of, what vegetables have you got lying around?" According to the laws, like-father-like-son, like-mother-like-daughter, all descendants of the Latin race have tomatoes, onions, sweet peppers, eggplant, and garlic, lying within their grasp at all times. For the perfectionist, a more precise recipe depends on which Roman ancestor you are wired into. The important thing is to use a lot of tomatoes. You should put in some cut up eggplant and be generous with the onion slices and chopped sweet peppers. After you have cooked the veggies in a blob of olive oil you may fine tune the mixture with garlic, oregano, sugar, pepper and salt to match the patient's desires. When this brew starts to emit beautiful aromas, you may add some beef broth.

Cuisine Après Dentist

🦷

This liquid dilution is a recent modification of an old recipe and is designed specifically for the tooth sufferer. The ratatouille, in this way, becomes the essence of flexibility. It can be fitted to a wide range of teething abilities as shown in the following tabulation.

The Roman Ratatouille Remedy

⇒⇒⇒⇒⇒⇒⇒⇒⇒⇒⇒⇒⇒

TOOTH-DENTAL CONDITION	**RECOMMENDED PREPARATION**
Basket Case...............................	*Tepid thin soup, i.e. remove all veggies and serve broth at body temperature with ample condolences*
One step removed from B.C........	*Same as B.C. except dunked bread may be added; use only half the condolences*
One Big Tooth Filling...................	*Full recipe, retain all vegetables, bread without crust, 1/4 tablespoon condolences*
Check up only, No Extractions, No Fillings.................................	*Forget Ratatouille, get out the cowboy steaks*

IF YOU ARE MORE COMFORTABLE WITH A FORMAL RECIPE TRY THE FOLLOWING.

ℛ ATATOUILLE

※※※※※

FOR 4 SERVINGS YOU NEED:

1 Large ONION, peeled and sliced

1 Large SWEET PEPPER , cut in pieces after

removing stem and core

2 GARLIC CLOVES, peeled and minced

2 cups cut-up EGGPLANT, peeled

1 cup ZUCCHINI, leave peel on and slice

1 Can (10 oz.), whole, peeled TOMATOES

include liquid (or 6 medium fresh tomatoes, cut up)

2 cups BEEF BROTH

1 teaspoon THYME

3 tablespoons OLIVE OIL

1/2 tablespoon SUGAR if you use fresh tomatoes

SALT and PEPPER to taste

2 or 3 tablespoons BURGUNDY WINE

---

*H*eat the oil in a deep skillet and add all vegetables including the garlic. Cook on low heat and stir the mixture frequently until the onions have softened (about 20 minutes). Add the beef broth and the thyme while continuing to stir occasionally (another 10 minutes). Then, add the wine, a few stirs, and about 5 minutes more.

Taste, add pepper and salt if you must, and stir. While you're sipping the results of your stirring work, read the following stirring story of an early ratatouille.

We have been referring to this dish as Roman Ratatouille imply-ing that it is a first cousin of Italian spaghetti. In truth Julius Caesar, a very old Italian, discovered it during one of his working vacations in an ancient place called Gaul. Caesar's Roman legions were win-tering in an area that later became known as Nice, France. It was a nice place then and it is a nice place today. It also happens to be the same place that gave birth to *SALAD NIÇOISE*.

In Roman-invasion days it was customary for the host country to supply the invading army with three meals a day. Since there was a war going on, meat was in short supply. The local green grocers scrounged some nightshade vegetables (vegetables which are stolen from poor farmers on moonless nights) and cooked up a meatless stew. Particular attention was directed to the stirring of the pot while the contents were stewing. If a vegetable was allowed to burn because of lack of stirring the ladle operator received an all-expense trip to Rome where he, or she, was presented to the lions in the Coliseum as an hors d'oeuvre. To stir was and is essential; so essential that the name ratatouille derived from the French verb *touiller,* meaning to stir.

Some latter-day residents of Gaul (called French Chefs) insist that to make a ratatouille properly each vegetable should be cooked sep-arately with its own selected herb. Then, the cook carefully mixes the six separately cooked vegetables into a single stew kettle (obviously an idea started by a pots and pans salesperson). My sister had a quick method for disposing of the six pan method: "You dirty up six of my pans to make one stew, you wash and dry six pans, and clean up the mess you made in the kitchen too!"

**THE ONLY SURE THINGS IN THIS LIFE ARE:
DEATH AND TAXES, TOOTHACHES
AND "WHEN DO WE EAT?"**

Chapter 4

Soup! What Else?

Grab a pad and pencil. Make yourself a badge printed with large letters saying *PRESS-INTERVIEW*, and you, all by yourself, can determine the actual eating habits of the average citizen after dentistry. Rather than asking the "average person on Main Street", which has been found to be quite hazardous in many parts of the "civilized" world, position yourself at the outside door of the dentist's office. As each person comes out get in step with them. Staying about an arm's length away, call out politely, "Pardon me, but could you tell me what you are planning to eat following this dental visit?" After you have screened out the offensive answers like, "Beat it before I punch you in the teeth," or, "Beat it before I scream and then punch you in the teeth," you will probably learn that most people will say, "Soup!" A few individuals will add, "What else?" What-else people should feel free to proceed directly to the next chapter where we will come to grips with "what-else" without mincing words, just food.

If you like to fool around with numbers and statistics, and if you are trying to strain out the "soup what else" question, try the same survey on different days of the week. We are all familiar with the astrological concept that Mondays are inherently worse than Fridays. This can be very true in dental matters.

During this part of the questioning it is interesting to probe other mood setting conditions like the weather, for example, is it rainy-gloomy or sunny-bright. In order to save you a lot of time and trouble, here are some typical results gathered from earlier studies:

DAY OF THE WEEK & WEATHER	RESPONSES ON LEAVING DENTIST OFFICE
Monday, Rain	8 out of 10 Soup (2 "WHAT ELSE ?")
Tuesday, Windy	9 out of 10 Soup (1 "GO AWAY")
Wednesday, Clear	7 out of 10 Soup (3 "MAYBE")
Thursday, So So	6 out of 10 Soup (4 "IN A HURRY")
Friday, Warm & Sunny ...	5 out of 10 Soup (5 "TGIF")

*F*or the sake of introducing the next recipe let's say it's Monday, it's raining, and you're headed homeward from the dentist. The soup du jour has got to be apple curry. Actually, the full name of this tasty dish is: *RAINY MONDAY'S APPLE ONION CURRY AFTER DENTIST SOUP.*

In Tasmania, where good apples are plentiful, it is said that this healing broth is used to treat acne, ague, and angina; further proof that an apple a day, in one form or another, keeps the doctor on the golf course. In checking this story for universal acceptance it has been found that New Englanders peel their apples a little differently. Some Bay Staters (those who have lived in Massachusetts for four or more generations) say that Johnny Appleseed's Portuguese grandfather introduced curry powder to second generation Pilgrims who were suffering from poor tooth genes because their parents had not flossed while they were coming across on the Mayflower.

Unrecognized historians tell us that this après dentist delight was conceived at Plymouth Rock on the 27th anniversary of the first Thanksgiving. Naturally in New England, the soup is made a little thicker so that a spoon can float on the surface. It is then called Apple Curry Chowder.

*A*PPLE *C*URRY *S*OUP

FOR 4 SERVINGS YOU NEED:

4 APPLES, core, peel, and cut in small pieces

4 medium ONIONS, skin removed and finely chopped

2 tablespoons SUGAR

4 cups BEEF BROTH

3 level teaspoons CURRY powder

2 cups CREAM, or HALF & HALF, or MILK

---

*P*ut all of the ingredients except the Curry powder and the Milk into a medium size pan and bring to a boil. Cover the pan, reduce the heat, and simmer for 25 minutes, stirring occasionally.

At this magical moment when the apples and onions are soft and vulnerable, carefully stir in the curry powder. WARNING! Curry powder is like a sweet spiced wine, a tad can titillate but a slather can slaughter. If you are timid about this herb from the Indies, try 1 teaspoon and then add more according to what the end of your tongue tells you.

Next, add the cream or milk, stir vigorously with a whisk, and continue on low heat for about 3 to 5 minutes. After adding the MILK, DO NOT ALLOW THE MIXTURE TO BOIL. Serve hot.

Tuesday is so near Monday that it sometimes feels like another gloom day. Should your appointment fall on Tuesday try a mood swing Swiss onion soup. This backbone building broth is often the main course at supper in many mountain monasteries. One folklore version traces its origin back to a group of French individualists who were trying to escape two things, religious persecution and French onion soup. They had too often become mired in a sticky, cloying morass of cheese that enshrouds some versions of this soup-with-onion.

The Swiss version consists of just three parts: a lot of sweet onions with paprika, a generous amount of good beef stock, and a thickening agent tempered with a little bit of beer.

$\mathscr{S}$WISS $\mathscr{O}$NION $\mathscr{S}$OUP

FOR 4 SERVINGS YOU NEED:

*2 pounds ONIONS (about 5 medium size) peeled
and sliced very thin*

4 tablespoons BUTTER

4 tablespoons OLIVE OIL

1 1/2 teaspoons PAPRIKA

6 cups BEEF BROTH

For the thickener:

3/4 cup FLOUR

1/2 cup VEGETABLE OIL

For the fine tuning:

1 cup BEER, optional

Here is what you do:

*M*elt butter with the olive oil in a heavy soup pot, Dutch oven, or deep skillet. Add onions and cook slowly, stirring often with a wooden spoon until the onion rings are soft. Sprinkle the paprika over the onions and continue stirring. The onions will take on a color that artists describe as sienna, a beautiful shade of color like the desert sands. Pour in beef broth and allow to simmer while you make the thickener that European cooks call a *roux*.

Roux: Heat the vegetable oil in a separate skillet and then add the flour while stirring with a whisk. The short-term goal is to produce a liquid that is evenly browned and very smooth. An engineer would say it has a uniform viscosity. Your favorite "old country" cook would call it "free flowing" like extra virgin olive oil. Slowly add this roux to the onion-beef broth. The slower you pour in the roux the less the oil will splatter when it meets the water in the broth. Keep the wooden spoon or whisk moving through the blending liquids.

Add such amounts of pepper and salt as you feel comfortable with. Remember, most prepared beef broths have some salt included. A teaspoon of ground celery seed and a pinch of red pepper can be administered at this point if you feel adventurous.

Cover the pot and let it simmer for 2 hours. During this time continue that important part of your therapy, for example: You can catch up on your yoga, relaxation response, or transcendental telepathy. Reading the comic pages is recommended for those who are into more basic mind-controlling escapism. Interrupt these reveries every few minutes to stir, and inhale, and sample the simmering mixture. WARNING: During this two-hour inhaling, tasting period, the quantity, 4 servings, has been known to diminish to 2 servings. Just before serving whatever is left add the optional beer and simmer for

another 2 or 3 minutes. Pour into preheated bowls. Add a sprinkle of Parmesan cheese, and a sprig of parsley.

The optimist looks at Wednesday as only two days to go till the week end. The pessimists are still struggling with the Monday-Tuesday hangover. Many oriental philosophies stress conversion to optimism. There is, they say, another life to come. For example, if you are not happy with your station in this present life, hang on, you may get another chance next time as a bird, butterfly, or a bullfrog. Then, speaking of eating, you can catch up on your birdseed, nectar and bugs. Meantime, it is Wednesday and you are just leaving the dentist's office. Try a page from the Asian ascetics who usually managed to harbor a good cook somewhere in the refectory. Consider the Chinese soup, Ching T'an (Translation: clear, pure, simple). Such food can act as a soothing salve to some of life's abrasive problems. Start with very lean pork or beef or chicken; leftover meat also works very well.

C LEAR *P* URE *S* IMPLE *C* HINESE *S* OUP

FOR EACH PARTICIPANT USE:

2 tablespoons lean PORK, BEEF, or CHICKEN cut up into
small bits about the size of the eraser on your lead pencil
PLACE MEAT PIECES IN A BOWL AND STIR IN
1 teaspoon SOY SAUCE
1 teaspoon CORNSTARCH

*S*tir and stab the meat with a fork, using another fork to remove any impaled morsels. While this marination process is proceeding fire up a burner on the stove, and bring to boil in a saucepan 1 cup *CHICKEN BROTH*. Add the meat plus any unabsorbed sauce, and adjust the heat to a lively simmer, continuing for ten minutes. Add a pinch of pepper and stir. After another minute or two, pour into a small bowl and, if you want to go first class, float a thin slice of lemon or a mushroom sliver on top of the simmering liquid.

Thursday, whether sunny and bright or cold and bitter, can be manhandled or woman-coddled by thinking cozy warm Bavarian potato soup. The starter liquid can be a vegetarian, a chicken, or a beef broth laced with bubbling well-cooked potatoes. It is not uncommon to drop in a bit of ground sausage or a bratwurst if your dietary boundaries include a romp outside of the vegetable-only territory.

*T*OOTH-*F*RIENDLY *B*AVARIAN *P*OTATO *S*OUP

2 SERVINGS:

2 medium POTATOES, peeled and sliced
2 cups CHICKEN BROTH
2 ONIONS, peeled and chopped
1 pinch of SALT, if you must
1 small, cooked SAUSAGE cut up into small bits and pieces

*P*ut all of the above into a pan and bring contents to a boil. Reduce heat and simmer for 20 minutes or until the potatoes and onions are soft. Mash the potatoes and what remains of the onion and sausage with a potato masher.

Using a whisk beat in:

1 or 2 grinds of PEPPER
1/4 teaspoon of CHERVIL
1 teaspoon chopped PARSLEY
2 tablespoons of LIGHT CREAM or SKIM MILK, your choice
Serve hot and smile.

---

*F*riday is, "Hey, I made it through the week," party day. So, fiesta your Friday with a good gazpacho. This is a great, "I'm out of here" soup which you start like a party, mild and cool, and if you want to heat it up, temperature-wise or chili-pepper-wise, you can choose to do it without giving your weekend a hangover. If this is one of those days when time is of the essence you can be sitting at table with your gazpacho in less than 5 minutes, assuming that you have the ingredients lying before you on the kitchen counter. If this recipe makes too much for your appetite, fret not, it stores well in the refrigerator and will taste great even when that tooth is not bothering you.

GAZPACHO SOUP
OF
THE SOUTHWEST

FOR 2 SERVINGS:

1 TOMATO stemmed and quartered

1/2 sweet green PEPPER

1 RADISH

1 stalk CELERY

4 slices of CUCUMBER

3 SCALLIONS (or 1/2 medium ONION), remove skin and roots

1 small peeled CLOVE GARLIC

2 cups TOMATO JUICE

1 teaspoon LEMON or LIME JUICE

2 teaspoons VINEGAR

2 tablespoons OLIVE or VEGETABLE OIL

1 teaspoon WORCESTERSHIRE SAUCE

4 ICE CUBES

Put all of the above into a blender and run on "chop" cycle until the particle size matches your teething abilities. Those of you who have been brought up in the Southwestern part of the North American Continent, or Mexico, or Central America may now wish to add your daily ration of hot chili peppers. As for the rest of you: If your taste buds say, "Come on, a little more snap," add a dash of McIlhenny's Tabasco Sauce.

Saturday is a different day and demands a different soup. Fruit soups are different and merit a try from those who haven't indulged. Like bikinis some people look good in a fruit soup, or more correctly stated, a fruit soup looks good on most people. Summertime brings out the best in locally grown fruit and a summer romance with a fruit soup can last through the fall and winter. Just for fun put the following "mixes" in a saucepan:

COOL SUMMERY FRUIT SOUP

FOR 4 SERVINGS:

1 cup WATER

1 cup RED WINE

1 quart FRESH STRAWBERRIES, hulled and pureed or hulled and chopped

1/2 cup SUGAR, if wine is tart; use 2 tablespoons sugar if wine is sweet

1 tablespoon LEMON or LIME JUICE

1/4 teaspoon ground CINNAMON

---

*S*tir together all of the above in a saucepan. Cover and simmer for 15 minutes. Let cool and give the mixture some refrigerator time before serving (1 hour minimum). This makes 4 servings and into each portion fold in a generous tablespoon of Cool Whip. For the daring, try a tablespoon of vanilla ice cream and stir until your gums tolerate the coolness.

If you have waited until the frost is on the pumpkin to make this fresh fruit, summer soup then you must proceed directly to the frozen goods section and acquire one package of frozen strawberries. Thaw the berries and "go for it" as if it were June in January. Some cooks in Wisconsin have been known to substitute a can of cherries plus a can of blueberries. When using frozen or canned fruit, if package shows that sugar has been included, reduce the recipe sugar accordingly.

Chickens have been with us a very long time. Buried deep in a place called legend is the idea that Noah, being without a calendar while sailing his ark in a multi-day rainstorm, relied on the rooster to count the passing days. Both the Phoenician and the Polynesian sailors counted their chickens both before and after each voyage. After the chickens had performed their waterborne duties (the male version crowing at dawn whether it was cloudy or clear, and the females providing the "where-with-all" for omelets or scrambled) the time came when the chicken itself came "a fowl" of the pot. Considering the full spectrum of herb additives as well as an option of rice or noodles, chicken soup can provide an ersatz penicillin for any day of the week, and always on Sunday.

Robinson Crusoe, a sailor of fictional repute, found himself stranded on an island with one chicken, a beach full of clams, and a growling stomach. Reducing the chicken to broth and straining the sand out of the clams' liquid he came up with nourishment for himself and his tooth-ailing man, Friday. You can do just as well and you don't necessarily have to start with a live chicken.

ROBINSON CRUSOE'S

CLAM TOMATO "BISKY" BROTH

2 SERVINGS:

Put the following in a medium pan:
2 cups CHICKEN BROTH
1 cup CLAM LIQUID
(Like Scotch whiskey, clam liquid now comes in a bottle)
1/2 cup CANNED TOMATOES
1/2 teaspoon finely chopped OREGANO
1/2 teaspoon finely chopped BASIL

While heating to a near boil stir rapidly with a whisk. You can add salt and pepper but I wouldn't advise adding very much. Simmer for 5 minutes to allow the flavors to get acquainted. The term "Bisky Broth" claims two parents. One is the slang version of BISQUE and the other is a terse description of what you can do with a dunking biscuit in this broth.

Mr. Crusoe always served this concoction in a scallop shell.

It is perfectly legal to make this soup on Tuesday except in Massachusetts where the mixing of tomatoes with clams is considered a crime punishable by expulsion to the state of Rhode Island.

ADMIRAL PERRY EXPLAINING TO HIS
GALLEY CHIEF WHY HE IS ORDERING
SOUP: "I HAVE NOT YET BEGUN TO BITE."

Chapter 5

New Aspects To Aspic
With A Side Trip To Mousse - Land

An aspic may be described in two words, SOLID SOUP. All the goodness of a flavorful broth can be built into an aspic. Like its cousin, the mousse, it deserves a special place with sensitive teeth. A tasty mousse can fool your gums into thinking that you are almost chewing.

Folk medicine teaches that the term *aspic* came from a plant, the *epic*, which was used in the treatment of snakebite in that sensuous area of Provence where the French romantics wet their feet in the Mediterranean. It has been said that the many colors of a properly prepared aspic resemble the shimmery shades of an asp, the snake that undid Cleopatra while she was barging up the Nile with Mark Anthony instead of a paddle.

**TOO BAD THAT CLEO DIDN'T TRY A
GOOD ASPIC BEFORE TURNING ON THE ASP.**

The aspic was first used as a side order to the main dish. It was often hidden away in the salad section of the cookbook. In today's nutritional approach to eating, the aspic can become the centerpiece in your candlelight supper. An aspic salad can be at the top of your eating pyramid. All four sides, meat, vegetable, fish, and fruit should be explored for a square meal.

An easy way to begin aspics is to borrow the menu from ocean-going cooks. Most ship-riding chefs have learned about fussy eaters when a rocking boat sends appetites "over the side." One remedy is a light beef broth, with a dollop of sherry wine. This can have restorative powers. In aspic form it can be a tooth pacifier.

BEEF - SHERRY ASPIC

FOR 2 PEOPLE YOU NEED:

1 packet unflavored GELATIN
2 tablespoons cold WATER
1 can (13 3/4 oz.) BEEF BROTH
1/4 cup dry SHERRY WINE

S prinkle the contents of 1 packet of unflavored gelatin over 2 tablespoons cold water in a small saucepan. After a few minutes a gel will form. Then, stir in 1 can beef broth and 1/4 cup of sherry wine. Cook over medium heat, stirring until the gelatin has dissolved. Remove from heat and allow to cool. The cooling can be expedited by placing the pan into a larger bowl of water with ice cubes. A water-filled kitchen sink also works well as a cooler. Stir the broth mixture until it has come back to room temperature, then place this precious cargo in the refrigerator until the mixture gels. When this occurs, usually after about an hour, take the pan out and break up the contents with a few stirs with a spoon and taste and enjoy and finish your aspic.

Tomato juice is an old standby when it comes to aspics. But you need not restrict your diet to this one vegetable. You can do your A, B, C's, asparagus, broccoli and cucumbers; or the whole garden plot with a can of V-8 juice. Add some gelatin mix, a dash of lemon juice, and a bit of what a mother hen calls "setting time." You can make a healthy, "look Ma, no teeth" snack. If you want to touch your taste buds with a haunting flavor mince in a bit of the salad vegetable called anise. If you want more "zing" add a tad of Tabasco or Worcestershire sauce.

Once upon a recipe, the meat derived aspic section of the nice housekeeping cookbook was pretty much limited to jellied consomme. Today no one with handicapped teeth should be denied the right to savor a New Zealand lamb aspic, an American BLT aspic, or a French beef burgundy aspic.

The original beef burgundy, *Boeuf Bourguignon,* was a many-layer labor of love, with a scheduled prep time of three to five hours. A briefer version has been "aspicked" into plain English as follows:

*B*EEF *B*URGUNDY *A*SPIC

FOR 4 SMALL OR 2 "BIG" SERVINGS:

**THINK ABOUT A 3-ACT PLAY IN WHICH YOU HAVE
THE LEADING ROLE.**

Act I

SCENE 1

A KITCHEN — A TALENTED CHEF (YOU) WITH:

1 cup ROAST BEEF, lean, cooked, shredded

(look in deli section of Supermarket)

2 heaping tablespoons ONION, finely minced

2 small CARROTS, minced

2 MUSHROOMS, sliced

2 small SHALLOTS, minced

1 clove GARLIC, mashed and minced

2 cups BEEF BROTH (or 1 can, 13 3/4 oz.)

1 cup BURGUNDY

2 tablespoons COGNAC

If you're in a hurry, toss beef and vegetables into a food processor and give the cutting blades a few whirls, just enough to reduce the contents to small pieces.

Put the minced beef and vegetables, colorful wine and cognac into a suitable pan. Bring to a boil, reduce heat, cover with a lid, and allow to simmer for about 40 minutes. Meanwhile:

Act I, Scene II

SAME KITCHEN, SAME CHEF CHARACTER

1 cup WHITE CABBAGE, shred or chop in small pieces
1 cup RED CABBAGE, shred or chop in small pieces
2 cups BEEF BROTH (or 1 can, 13 3/4 oz.)

Place the chopped cabbage and the beef broth in a 1 or 2 quart pan, cover, bring and keep at a low simmer. Meanwhile:

Act I, Scene III

STILL SAME KITCHEN, SAME CAST

1 envelope unflavored GELATIN
2 tablespoons COLD WATER

Sprinkle the envelope of unflavored gelatin over the 2 tablespoons of water which have been placed in a 2-quart pan. Allow a gel to form, and when the beef and veggies, which have been simmering in another pan, have completed their cooking time (about 40 minutes) add them to the gel and stir until well mixed.

Heat the mixture until it comes to a boil. Remove from the heat and allow to cool. Steal a taste and add such pepper and salt as you might require. When it has neared room temperature place the pan in the refrigerator and allow to gel, about 1 to 2 hours.

Act II
SCENES 1, 2, AND 3

At this point in a "for real" play the hero/heroine would step to the refrigerator and pull out a just finished beef burgundy to a background of Ohs and Ahs. Since your stagehand did not previously prepare the "other" finished dish you will have to wait for the allotted gel time. Meantime, check to see how the cabbage is doing. Keep it on low simmer and don't let it run dry. Add some water if necessary. The next act starts when the gel gels.

Act III
THE BIG SCENE

Remove the cabbage with a slotted spoon and divide it among the four serving bowls. Take the gel from the refrigerator and chop it, just a little, with a wooden spoon. Place your "burgundy" on the cabbage leaves. If you are going "all out" use sherbet glasses and top with a sprig of parsley.

In the fin and shell game try a bit of minced clams, shrimp, or scallops in your taste-of-the-sea aspic. Get your hooks into a good fish market or harvest a succulent sample from a salmon farm.

If you want to lighten up your food even more, think of a soft, tooth-friendly mousse, a French expression meaning froth and foam.

$\mathscr{S}$ALMON $\mathscr{M}$OUSSE

FOR 4 SERVINGS:

2 envelopes unflavored GELATIN
1 can SALMON (15 1/2 oz.)
1 small ONION, peeled
1 stalk CELERY
3 or 4 slices of CUCUMBER
3/4 cup MAYONNAISE
1 cup whipping or heavy CREAM
1 1/2 tablespoons LEMON JUICE
1 teaspoon DILL WEED,
(You may substitute 2 teaspoons juice from the pickle jar)
1 teaspoon PARSLEY
3 or 4 OLIVES (green, black, stuffed, whatever — but no pits)
Salt to taste, suggest not more than 1/2 teaspoon

*P*our the liquid from the can of salmon into a measuring cup and add room temperature water to make 1 cup. Put this liquid in a medium saucepan and sprinkle the gelatin over the surface. After a few minutes place the pan on low heat and stir. Continue for about 5 minutes until all gelatin is completely dissolved.

In a food processor or blender, fine-chop all of the remaining ingredients and add them to the gelatin mixture. Stir well to be sure that the gelatin is well distributed. Pour into a serving bowl and chill in the refrigerator until firm. Many cooks like to pour the salmon mixture into a fish shaped mold and then, after the mixture has gelled, the mold is placed momentarily in a pan of hot water to aid in the release of the mousse from the mold. Turn the mold upside down and drop the mousse onto a bed of lettuce.

Some college fraternities are reputed to have used these molds with goldfish placed in the bottom prior to the addition of the salmon mixture. A number of reliable fish mongers have expressed the opinion that the salmon/goldfish species should neither be mixed together or eaten together. That is to say, goldfish swallowers and salmon lovers should be separated by a high fence at all times.

If you want to keep this mousse thing going through dessert, put together a cranberry mousse.

CRANBERRY MOUSSE

FOR 6 SERVINGS:

1 cup CRANBERRY JUICE
1 package (3 oz.) RASPBERRY OR STRAWBERRY FLAVORED GELATIN
1 can (16 oz.) whole berry CRANBERRY SAUCE
1 cup whipped HEAVY CREAM (or Cool Whip)

———

*H*eat the cranberry juice to boiling in a saucepan and stir in the gelatin until it is dissolved. Add the cranberry sauce and stir until evenly distributed. Chill until the mixture thickens. Fold in the whipped cream (save a few spoonfuls for decoration), and pour into serving dishes. Chill in the fridge until firm. When serving decorate the top with a touch of whipped cream. You could also add a cherry or a strawberry on the top like it was "riding in a creamy cloud."

QUICK MOUSSE

Where minimum preparation time is important here is instant mousse gratification. Use the Jell-O gelatin snack cups available in most supermarkets. For each eater, spoon out the contents of one 3 1/2 oz. cup into a cereal bowl and add one tablespoon of Cool Whip and three or four chopped strawberries. Stir with a spoon and

let it melt in your mouth. If strawberries are a no-show, call in the blueberries, boysenberries, or blackberries, or for berry-less days, a slice or two of a well-ripened banana will do nicely.

She was the quintessence of cutting wit. She could gather a group at a cocktail party faster than Harrison Ford could round up a herd of buffalo for a Western movie. On and on she went regaling her listeners with: "I was simply enchanted with the good taste of perfection which said to me, 'Good breeding.' Finally I told her, this is for me. This is a mousse I could fall in love with." An enraptured gentleman leaned forward and asked: "Pearl, Darling . . . er . . . please share the recipe for this tasty mousse." She turned her head slowly in the direction of the question, and noticing the light glistening from the bald head of the inquirer, she replied: "My dear Peter, you couldn't possibly fall in love with my mousse. I am speaking of the mousse my hairdresser uses."

> AN ASPIC THAT YOU FALL IN LOVE
> WITH CAN BE A DEAR MOUSSE,
> BUT A MOOSE MOUSSE IS
> AN AWFUL LOT OF
> DEER TROUBLE.

Chapter 6

Soft Sandwiches In
Seven Languages

The earliest people to live on our planet were concerned with five basic activities: (1) Finding something to eat

(2) Eating

(3) Doing what you have to do after you eat

(4) Sleeping

(5) Procreating

(Not necessarily in that order)

When they hunted for food, they concentrated on hunting for food. When they ate, they ate. For a very long time these basic tasks filled up all of the available hours between one sunset and the next. Then came the moment when someone found that they could do two things at the same time; "One giant step for mankind." Actually the idea was probably conceived by a Mrs. Cave Lady who suggested to a Mr. Cave Man that when he went out to find a mastodon steak for dinner would he please at the same time take out the garbage bones from last night. History, however, waited until the eighteenth century to provide an eating device that would allow the common citizen to stuff one's face while performing other tasks. This eating device may be aptly described as: "HEY! I'm too busy to stop for lunch. Let's

grab a sandwich." This layered arrangement of bread slices and fill-
ings requires only one of our two hands for the operation of down-
loading food (a fifty percent reduction in the labor requirements over
earlier two-handed techniques). One hand now becomes available to
talk with, doodle with, or participate in some totally independent
activity. Credit for contriving this ingenious invention goes to a John
Montagu, one of the rogues of the Merry Old England period.
Montagu, in the middle of a winning streak at the game of dice, could
not leave the gaming table for the dining table. Without missing a
throw of the cubes, he bade his cook to fetch a slice of game hen with
a slab of bread rolled around it. You could say it was a case of being
on a roll and eating one too. The local gentry started to refer to this
one-handed meal as a "roller." However, Montagu's public-relations,
"spin doctors," came up with the idea that since John Montagu was
the fourth earl of a land-grabbed area called Sandwich, the "roller"
should henceforth be designated the "sandwich."

A few years later Captain Cook, on one of his Pacific swing-a-
bouts, came across some exotic islands in the middle of nowhere and
staked a claim for the English crown specifying the name to be the
Sandwich Islands (later called Hawaii). The logbooks show that on
Cook's next trip to the Sandwich Islands he got into a misunder-
standing with the natives and literally lost his head. This was probably one of the earliest examples in history of the locals resisting a fast-
food franchise.

Today the word sandwich suggests the dovetailing of a piece of
bread with a food that isn't bread: dainty Danish deviled ham on
dainty dabs of decrusted bread; cream cheese on challah; crabs on
crumpets; open face with beef au jus; meatballs in a pocket; salamis
on a hero; a refrigerator in a Dagwood.

As the vertical dimension of the sandwich grows, the difficulty of chewing it by the tooth impaired increases by leaps and bounds. Let's take out the problem part and order a soft creamy Scandinavian sardine sandwich.

$\mathscr{S}$OFT $\mathscr{S}$CANDINAVIAN $\mathscr{S}$ARDINE $\mathscr{S}$ANDWICH

2 SERVINGS

2 EGGS, hard boiled, shells removed, and mashed with a fork

1 can, (4 3/8 oz.) SARDINES, drained and mashed

2 tablespoons BUTTER or OLEO

1 slice toasted BREAD, cut up in small cubes

2 slices BREAD, remove crust

3/4 cup HALF & HALF or MILK

1/2 teaspoon PAPRIKA

1/4 to 1/2 teaspoon CURRY POWDER, taste it as you go

SALT to taste

$\mathcal{M}$elt butter or oleo in a medium saucepan. Add eggs, sardines, milk, and spices while stirring. Add the cut-up toast and adjust heat to get mixture as hot as possible without boiling. Place a slice of crustless bread in the bottom of a serving dish and spoon on the creamy sardines.

Note: The "soupiness" of the creamy sardines may be adjusted to your tooth condition by adding more or less milk. Some people pour a small amount of milk onto the bread before adding the sardine mixture. This softens the bread and by using a seedless rye your creamy sardines will take on a "deli" flavor.

If you have joined the "I like salsa" crowd, substitute 1 tablespoon of salsa for the paprika and curry powder.

*C*HEESE *S*ANDWICH *S*OUP

❦❦❦❦❦❦
FOR EACH PERSON

2 thin pieces TOAST
3 tablespoons grated Cheddar or Swiss CHEESE
1 cup very warm MILK
Pinch NUTMEG

*I*n a warmed and wide bowl place one piece of toast. Sprinkle the cheese evenly over the toast. Place the second piece of toast over the cheese. Add the nutmeg to the heated milk and pour over the toast. This recipe is well suited to microwave heating.

Admittedly it may require both hands to walk around eating this kind of "sandwich." However, by waving your spoon between slurps you can make your point emphatically. Seeking more candidates for the title of soft sandwich, think of a little soft cheese sandwiched all around with "munchable" dough. Some cooks call it manicotti. It could suggest a ravioli, a gnocchi or a tortellini. Even at the Ritz-Carlton they allow you lots of sauce on your ravioli, over the top and around the sides. Don't try that at the Ritz on a menu-advertised luncheon sandwich.

The soft sandwich equivalents in Tel Aviv could be blintzes and knishes, in Paris the crepe, the tiropetakia in Athens, the golombki in Gdansk. In Beijing it could be a softened egg roll. In Tijuana a soft taco dunked in gazpacho soup and sometimes snickeringly stipulated as a Senorita Sandwich because it has a soft shoulder.

✤ CHEESE BLINTZ ✤
FOR TWO

BLINTZ

1/2 cup FLOUR
1 pinch SALT
1 EGG, beaten
1 teaspoon COOKING OIL
1/2 cup SKIM MILK

BLINTZ FILLING

1 tablespoon YOGURT
1/2 teaspoon SUGAR
6 oz. CREAM CHEESE

Mix the flour and the salt. Add the egg and the oil and stir thoroughly with a whisk. Gradually add the milk and continue to whisk. Use about the same wrist motion that you would use if you were making pancakes. Pour about 2 tablespoons on a hot greased griddle and turn as soon as they appear to solidify. Remove as soon as they can be handled and store in a toaster oven (set to low) until you are ready to add the filling.

Mix the filling ingredients. Put a tablespoon of this filling in the center of each blintz and then roll the edges over like you were covering the baby. Press down the edges and return the packaged cheese to the griddle for just long enough to make it hold together or until it turns a very light brown. Remember we want them soft.

Theologians tell us that man does not live by bread alone. I agree. There has to be a woman involved. Otherwise, where's the panache? If woman or man, you are looking for an alternative to the usual crusted form of raised dough, try the popover. When you get inside

a proper popover it's warm and soft and tongue pleasing all over. They go well with a fruit jam, a soft cheese, or "just butter." You can make your own soft sandwich.

$\mathscr{P}$OPOVERS
≫•≫•≫

2 EGGS

1 cup FLOUR

1 cup MILK (skim milk is fine)

1/2 teaspoon SALT

$\mathcal{M}$ix thoroughly and pour into individual 5 or 6 oz. glass baking cups. Place in a cold oven and set to 450°F. Do not disturb for 30 minutes then sneak-a-peak and . . . Wow!

After Charles Lindbergh made his epic solo flight from New York to Paris he was asked about what kept him going for those interminable 33 hours. How could he stay awake to do all the demanding things he had to do to keep the plane flying on course? With the typical modesty of a real hero, Lindbergh spoke of the "famous" sandwiches which were handed to him just before takeoff that rainy, foggy, May 27, 1927, morning at Long Island, New York. He recalled saying to himself, "When I get over Newfoundland I'll have a sandwich. When I got to Newfoundland I told myself no, I'll wait till I get halfway across the Atlantic, and then, I promised myself, when I get over Ireland. I never ate the sandwiches but the idea of planning to eat the sandwiches kept me going."

THE EARL OF SANDWICH MAY HAVE BEEN A GREAT IMPRESARIO BUT IT TAKES A BROOKLYN DELI TO MAKE A REAL HERO.

Chapter 7

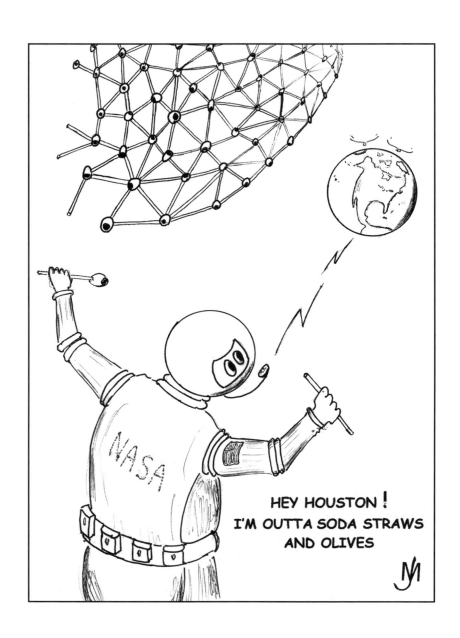

The Liquid Lunch Doesn't Have
To Be A Martini With Ensure

He was distinguished looking, tall, well-built, and dressed in a way that said foreign correspondent. It was too late for lunch and too early for cocktails. It was the hour of the High Tea. My wife and I were sitting in the lounge bar of the Peninsular Hotel, Hong Kong, after the cancellation of a sightseeing trip. We were filling time with one of our favorite games, pick out an occupant of a nearby table and deduce their occupation. Tall, well-built happened to have seated himself at a table where both of us could unobtrusively observe him. I was sure he was a foreign correspondent because of the self assured way he swept in, tossing a dark trench coat onto a nearby chair. He didn't even look at the coat landing on the chair. He knew it would land on the chair. In contrast my wife, with the impregnable reasoning that she just had a feeling, kept pushing the idea that he was a salesman. As his tea arrived, a peculiar thing happened. He reached into an inner pocket and brought out a silver case. It was about the size of a pencil box that I used to have in my early schooldays but my pencil box was not silver. He opened it and took out what looked like a glass thermometer. Damn! I thought. I'm wrong. He's a

doctor. Then, he attached a silvered mouth piece to what I thought was the thermometer, but now I could see it was actually a long plastic straw or maybe it was a glass straw.

My wife mused, "Do you suppose he's taking opium?"

Then, he inserted one end in the tea cup and the silvered end in his mouth. We could see the transit of the tea.

Tea time passed and leaving time came. Tall and well built went through a ritual of disassembling his silver-tipped straw, cleaning it and restoring it to its silver case. He turned in our direction, he beamed, and then he nodded. It was a signal that he knew that we knew; a silent acknowledgment that all three parties had participated, at least in spirit, in the straw-sipping session. At this point in time I was in favor of making a pronto exit. My wife preferred the fantasy: drop through a crack in the floor.

As he passed our table on his way to the exit he bowed graciously and asked: "How are you two enjoying your visit to our lovely city?" We were crushed; crushed by his ability to spot two foreigners who considered themselves to be well-camouflaged travelers. We blustered, "Great, wonderful." He filled the gap in the ensuing silence with, "Sensitive teeth, you know. My straw's a simply marvelous help after a visit to the dentist chap." Then he laid down an embossed business card and left. My wife cut through my foggy daze with, "What'zit say?" I picked up the card and handed it to her.

CHRISTOPHER BRAMBERLY III
Purveyor Of Plumbing Supplies
2205 Chinlee Lane
Kowloon, Hong Kong

❏***Question:*** *WHAT COULD BE WORSE THAN A TOOTHACHE?*
❏***Answer:*** *A TOOTHACHE WITH COLD AND FLU SYMPTOMS*

You know you have a problem when you have sinus with rhinitis, flu feeling and head reeling, sore throat plus stomach bloat, and your runny nose is adding to your tooth woes.

You can't talk so good and you can't hear so well. The rest of the human race removes itself like you have the plague. Well, in decibels of distress you do. Actually, you are probably a very fine person, when viewed from afar. You will be offered the consolation, *THIS IS NOT TERMINAL*. But, you wish it were. You want to go to bed but you can't get out of your torture-jacket. Your stomach is telling you it's upset with the way you're focusing on your head parts, mouthing aspirin, and guzzling TV, miracle drugs. Your tummy could be screaming because it's as empty as a spinach can after Popeye snacked.

On the premise, *FEED A COLD, STARVE A FEVER*, those with a temperature higher than 98.6° F should proceed directly to the nearest dispensary. The feverless, cold-symptom, tooth-aching reader should consider a stomach liner, insulation if you will. Coat the innards of your midsection and the reaches of your mind with a warm *liquid lunch.*

ℰELERY 𝒮OUP WITH A STRAW

*T*ake some condensed celery soup and your favorite salad croutons for a spin in the blender. Thin with a bit of water or milk and heat thoroughly. Then, cool to "your" temperature and try it with a straw. Men, if you think drinking with a straw will tarnish your

macho image, remember that many professional boxers use straws quite often, especially after a major bout in which their jaws have been pounded into chopped liver.

✠ OTHER SOULFUL STOMACH SUSTENANCE ✠

- STEAMY BEEF BROTH WITH A BIT OF SHERRY
- VERY WARM CIDER PLUS CLOVES AND NUTMEG
- HEATED CRANBERRY JUICE WITH CLOVES
AND A CINNAMON STICK

If you are fortunate you may find a "tube" cinnamon stick that can substitute for a straw. Sip the warm, cloved, cranberry juice and think about the old man who was living in the fall of his life in a country that was going through a fall in its life—Norway, 1940. The enemy soldiers had passed through the old man's village and taken most of his food. He had managed to stash away a little coffee and precious sugar. The soldiers found the sugar

As he pondered, "How will I drink my coffee without my sugar?" he noticed some rounded pebbles on his front walk. He washed two of the smaller stones and carefully placed them in his mouth between his lips and his front teeth. Then he slowly sipped the coffee through his pursed lips, through the stones, and imagined that it was the best tasting coffee ever. He dreamt of the war's end, and he dreamt of surviving, and he dreamt of springtime, and he could taste the sugar in the coffee that didn't have any sugar in it.

**SODA STRAWS AND TOOTHPICKS ARE GOOD FOR SOMETHING
BESIDES
BUILDING SPACE PLATFORMS.**

♣ ♣ ♣ ♣ ♣ ♣

Chapter 8

What Do Chefs Eat When They Have A Toothache?

Competition can be fierce in the restaurant business. One establishment that catered to families went the "extra mile" by keeping a supply of baby food on hand. When the kid noise became excessive, one of the waitresses put on an extra large chef's hat. The only way to describe the hat was to say that it was a very big hat, and it was a funny hat. Approaching the noisy table the server-turned-actress would make a bowl of rabbit-shaped baby food appear suddenly from under the hat. The young noise maker usually became so entranced with the distraction that a normal background noise level returned.

One day the cook had a toothache. He emptied a baby food jar and some onion juice in a saucepan that still had the remnants of Mornay sauce. When he turned his back the Mornay baby food had disappeared. The waitress with the hat had tasted it, all of it.

The next day they had a customer with a tooth problem. The waitress suggested a soup and puréed vegetables Mornay. The customer was pleased and no one knew the humble source of vegetables Mornay, except the waitress, the chef, and the trash collector.

Speaking of trash collection and the discreet disposal of food containers:

Guests were attacking the hors d'oeuvres in the living room. I retired to the kitchen to check on the stove's progress with dinner. Moments later, some of the guests came into the kitchen to compliment me on the hors d'oeuvres. I started to tell them how I make *SCRUMPTIOUS DIP* but I never got a chance because the guests were staring at the kitchen counter. "Oh damn!" I forgot to trash the empty cat food can; the *9 Lives* label stared at everyone in the room. And everyone knew we didn't have a cat. What everyone did not know was that on this particular evening I had agreed to feed the neighbors' cat while they were away.

With the passage of time I have learned to: (1) tolerate cats; (2) turn this menu-for-disaster into a humorous house tradition with each new unsuspecting guest: When a visitor comes into the kitchen during meal preparation and asks, "What can I do to help?" I hand them a can of cat food as I stir a pot and say, "Would you mind opening this can for me? I want to jazz up my Hungarian goulash."

Oh yes, the recipe for scrumptious dip:

SCRUMPTIOUS DIP
(the no-teeth-required hors d'oeuvre)

*I*n a small bowl, pour a tablespoon of sherry wine over four tablespoons of room temperature liver sausage (mashable liverwurst). Add two crushed saltine crackers and mix thoroughly with a fork. Spread this mixture on strips of well-ripened avocado.

In recent years we have asked many chefs in many kitchens what they eat when they have a toothache. Here are some appropriate answers straight from these sore jawed, scullery scholars: At the Fay Club where the doers and shakers of central Massachusetts meet, good food has been a tradition for three generations. In mid-twentieth century, a chef named Scott Thorsen was manning the pots and pans. He always provided a favorite soup and souffle for anyone suffering from tired teeth or general grumpiness. Scotty's stories were as famous as his tooth-friendly food.

In December 1911, the Norwegian explorer, Roald Amundsen was trying to reach the South Pole. Scott Thorsen, a young countryman of Amundsen was a member of the backup team standing by to launch a rescue effort if Amundsen and his party ran into trouble getting back to civilization. Amundsen made it back without help but with enough documentation to be acknowledged as the first human to actually reach the South Pole. Scott Thorsen returned and lived on to become a respected and much loved Chef in the heart of New England. It is an interesting juxtaposition of names. Amundsen beat out his rival in getting to the Pole by 20 days. The rival's name was Captain Scott, a renowned English polar explorer. When the whole story became known of Amundsen's triumph and Scott's tragic defeat (Scott's party froze to death in a snow-covered shelter) Scott Thorsen remembered that members of both polar expeditions carried hard biscuits and dunked them in their heated gruel to soften them because their teeth hurt so badly from the cold.

One of Scott Thorsen's successors at the Fay Club was Robert Holmes, who retained the standards of good food and consideration for the tooth impaired. Chef Holmes recommended facing a dental problem at mealtime with his wine-poached haddock or steamed

halibut. Other choices from his menu designed to be easy on the molars included a finely ground pork with cinnamon apples, and Basmati rice (most markets now carry this grain from India that can be prepared to come out very soft and tender). Another winner is his skinless bratwurst made tooth friendly by slowly simmering it in beer and adding a soft egg on the side.

Eggs have often provided a satisfying answer to the question, "What am I going to eat now?" At the Churchill Hotel in London, Swiss eggs are an old standby for touchy teeth.

$\mathscr{S}$WISS $\mathscr{E}$GGS

FOR 2 SERVINGS YOU NEED:

2 EGGS
2 tablespoons SOFT CREAM CHEESE
Dash of PEPPER

---

*T*he cheese should be allowed to come to room temperature so that it will disperse easily through the egg. A favored procedure is to break the eggs in a greased skillet and stir in the cream cheese just as if you were making scrambled eggs. The time of cooking and whether or not the egg is "turned over" can follow the eater's preference. A dash of pepper and a sprig of parsley makes the "presentation."

On the west coast of the U.S. where Chinese cooking first gained widespread American acceptance several chefs recommended egg foo yung. As one smiling cook in San Luis Obispo said: "Egg for young and old, with teeth or with no teeth."

EGG FOO (FU) YUNG

FOR 2 SERVINGS

(If you are very hungry double all ingredients):

2 EGGS

2 teaspoons finely chopped SCALLION

2 tablespoons finely chopped cooked HAM

2 tablespoons chopped BEAN SPROUTS

(canned sprouts are not as crunchy as fresh sprouts but are easier

for those in a delicate dental condition)

1 cup room temperature BEEF BROTH

2 teaspoons CORNSTARCH

2 teaspoons SOY SAUCE

2 teaspoons SUGAR

2 teaspoons VINEGAR

*B*reak the eggs and drop into a mixing bowl. Add the scallions, ham, bean sprouts, and stir until well mixed. Heat a small greased skillet and cook the egg batter using about 1/3 cup at a time. Turn over each patty as soon as the egg sets, before it becomes brown. Accumulate the patties in an oven with the temperature set to low. Put the serving plates in to warm up at the same time.

Meantime on a back burner in a saucepan mix together the room-temperature, beef broth and the cornstarch. Turn up the heat to a medium setting and let's see some real stirring. Add the soy sauce, sugar and vinegar and more stirring. When this sauce starts to bubble

and thicken reduce the heat and keep warm for serving. Place an egg patty on a heated plate, add a couple of tablespoons of the sauce, and garnish with an orange slice. If you are able to serve up four or more patties with sauce and garnish before an eater has read the morning paper's comic strips, give yourself a chef rating of four stars.

Omelets have always been a favorite with hungry dental casualties. One chef in the Bahamas suggested, for those eaters who are also concerned about cholesterol, "Order a three-egg soft omelet using the yolk of only one egg." We asked, "What happens to the leftover yolks?"

"Aha!" he replied with the question, "Do you know why they call it devil's food cake?"

At the Black Rose in Scottsdale, Arizona, Chef Robert Rosales introduced us to a broccoli souffle which was the epitome of lightness and subtlety. He said, however, when he mixed dental visits with eating his first choice was baked potato sour cream soup.

In Vincent's on Camelback Road in Phoenix, Arizona, Chef Vincent surprised everyone, especially the Yankees, when he went all out for his no-teeth-required lobster bisque. It was probably that touch of cilantro that put a southwestern twist on this wonderful Nova Scotian treat.

San Francisco boasts many fine restaurants ready, willing, and able to satisfy special needs. At Pastry on Post Street, the Rosenthal brothers cook a succulently softened salmon with a plum sauce and serve it on a bed of mashed potatoes. Pastry chef Janet Rikala adds a memorable finish with a frothy lemon cheesecake. One eater reported, "You can chew through this entire meal with your tongue and the roof of your mouth."

In Dallas, Texas, Dean Fearing, chef at The Mansion on Turtle

Creek, says that cheddar cheese soup has served him well since child-hood. What makes his cheese soup unique is the Texas seasonings melding smoothly into this traditionally Wisconsin dish.

Other suggestions from around the world have been gathered to form an alphabetical-geographical source of food ideas. You who are hungry and thirst for food that is tooth-nerve tolerant, here is your

Fantasy List:

Albuquerque, NM, Maria Teresa Restaurant, Old Town: *Gazpacho Soup*

Amarillo, TX, Jorge's Mexican Cafe: *Chile Rellenos + Margaritas*

Bar Harbor, ME: The Porcupine Grill: *Bouillabaisse*

Basil, Switzerland: Fiskhstube Zum Pfauen: *Quenilles Pike*

Beijing, China, Friendship Hotel: *Steamed Fish + Chinese Dumplings*

Berlin, Germany, Cafe Kransler: *Beef Tea + Dunking Brot + Soft Cheese*

Bermuda, The Pink Beach: *Conch Chowder with Sherry*

Boston, MA, Anthony's Pier 4: *Marinated Mushrooms +Popovers + Fish Chowder*

Boston, MA, Budapest: *Hungarian Goulash*

Chicago, IL, Biggs: *Tenderized Shrimp in Tomato Aspic*

Copenhagen, Denmark, Belle Terrace, Tivoli: *Tureen of the Sea*

Dublin, Ireland, Abbey Tavern (Howth): *Irish Stew*

Dublin, Ireland, Aisling at the Shelbourne: *Casserole of Prawns & Lobster*

Flagstaff, AZ, Little America: *Western Omelet*

Fryeburg, ME, Fryeburg Inn: *Eggs Any Style*

Glasglow, Scotland, The Drum & Monkey: *Lemon Fish Flan*

Grand Canyon, AZ, Phantom Ranch Canteen: *Hiker's Stew*

Cuisine Après Dentist

Helsinki, Finland, Walahalla: *Rapukeitto (Cray Fish Soup)*

Herman, MO, Stone Hill Winery Restaurant: *Kohl Suppe (Cabbage Soup)*

Hilton Head, SC, Hilton: *She Crab Soup*

Hong Kong, Jimmy's Kitchen: *Mulligatawny Soup*

Kona, Hawaii, Kona by the Sea: *Poached Mahi Mahi*

Kyota, Japan, Daiichi: *Suppon (Terrapin Broth) + Zosui (Rice)*

Leuven, Belgium, The Ramberg: *Consomme of Pigeon + Mushrooms*

London, England, Savoy: *Vichyssoise and Fruited Flan*

London, England, Simpsons: *Bubble and Squeak + Bangers*

London, England, Churchill Hotel: *Swiss Eggs + Tomato juice*

Mariposa, CA, The Hull House: *Beer Battered Mushrooms + Fettuccini Alfredo*

Memphis, TN, Peabody Hotel: *Sweetbreads*

Montery, CA, The Sardine Factory: *Seafood Chowder*

Moscow, Russia, National: *Crepes with Salmon, Caviar and Sour Cream*

New Orleans, LA, Brennan's: *Oyster Soup + Bananas Foster*

Naples, FL, Ritz-Carleton: *Cream of Jerusalem Artichoke Soup*

New York, NY, Luchow's: *Sauerbraten in Aspic*

New York, NY, Oscar at the Waldorf: *Souffle de Poisson*

Palm Beach, FL, The Breakers: *Borscht + Bagel Dunking*

Paradise Valley, AZ, Hermosa Inn (Lon's): *Salmon Mesquite + Horseradish Mashed Potatoes*

Paris, France, Maxim's: *Scallops a la Crevette*

Philadelphia, PA, Bookbinders: *Mock Turtle Soup + Crab Cakes*

Portland, ME, Boone's: *Finnan Haddie Newburg*

Quebec, Canada, Chateau Frontenac: Pea *Soup Acadian*

San Diego, CA, Coronado: *Sand Dabs sautèed in wine + Minced Herb Sauce*

San Juan, Puerto Rico, Ramero's: *Flower Shaped Peppers filled with Salmon Mousse*

Seattle, WA, Top of the Needle: *Dungeness Crab Newburg*

Sedona, AZ, The Heartline Cafe: *Corn, Bean, Squash Casserole*

St. Martin, (Caribbean), Oyster Pond Hotel: *Poached Red Snapper, Sauce Piquante*

Sturbridge, MA, The Public House: *Lobster Newburg*

Sydney, Australia, Bennelongs, Opera House: *Crab Bisque*

Taipei, Taiwan, Grand Hotel: *Hot and Sour Mandarin Soup*

Taos, NM, Roberto's: *Beans, Beans, Beans and Mariachi Band*

Tarpon Springs, FL, Louis Papa's: *Poached Pompano*

Texas, Any place except the Alamo: *Texas Chili*

Thule, Greenland, US Air Force Base: *Soft Omelette*

Tilton, NH, The Country Place, B&B: *Carrot Soup + Crepes with Maple Syrup*

Tokyo, Japan, Sardine Iwashiya: *Miso Soup + Sardine Burgers*

Tuscon, AZ, Ventana Canyon Resort: *Eggs Ranchero*

> **THE CAT THAT HAD NINE LIVES NEVER WENT TO THE DENTIST IT JUST ATE SCRUMPTIOUS DIP.**

Chapter 9

Smashed Potatoes
In Nine Flavors

If Adam and Eve had stuck to horticulture they might have set out to create the perfect food, the potato. Instead they chose to mess with the apple and the potato genes were left to their own devices. Eons later the spud turned up in South America. Nature's methods are often obscure but the results are wondrous. It is a fervent hope of many laypersons that pragmatic theologians and "archiving" archeologists will someday delay their Garden-of-Eden vs we-came-from-a-monkey argument long enough to determine why the potato did not turn up in the Euphrates region of Asia Minor, one of the theorized sites of the Garden of Eden. Instead it showed up in the land of the Incas along with a sun god and lots of monkeys. Another biblical, horticultural question that might be asked by the laity is, "Did Noah take along two potatoes when he loaded the ark?"

European civilization had to rely on the European explorers who had come to the Americas to grab gold but had returned, for the most part, with curios like potatoes and tomatoes. Later, back in Holland, the descendants of the early Dutch sailors are credited with improving the potato by developing better breeding strains with less

farming pains. Having done something for the eye with tulips, the Hollanders now targeted the palate with potatoes.

Horticulture continued to progress with pioneers like Luther Burbank, and progress reports from the Annual Burpee Seed Catalog. Today we can walk into any food emporium and choose from hundreds of potato derived foodstuffs. A New Yorker, to cite an instance, can not only pick up some potato pancake flour but can bag some Long Island potatoes freshly trucked in from Idaho.

While the northern Europeans were heavy on the potato their southern counterparts weighed in with improvements on the tomato. The progeny of the Italian and Spanish globetrotters concentrated on the red, vine fruit that had been brought back from the New World. Marco Polo had already taught his kinfolk how to make Chinese noodles, so the sires of Columbus were, you might say, olive ripe for developing spaghetti with tomato sauce, a very tooth-friendly repast.

More recently tomato plant research has been carried forward at the college which participated in the first American football game. The New Jersey University, Rutgers, has probably scored more points with its tomato skins than it has with its pigskins; no less a familiar sight than Campbell's tomato soup has benefited and pleased folks in over forty countries.

Potatoes, unlike tomatoes, have been much maligned in recent times. The potato has been accused of being a waistline expander. Nevertheless and notwithstanding, we love the potato. People who make their living keeping track of numerical curiosities tell us that the average American eats their equivalent weight in potatoes every 365 days. Yes, 126 pounds of fried, baked, boiled, mashed, or liquefied—the latter is sometimes called vodka.

Pseudo-reasoning could argue that each year the average weight of the average American will increase and therefore, the consumption

of potatoes will continue to spiral upward. Before we join this lynching mob to hang the innocent potato let us, as a last resort, call upon "just the facts ma'am." Analysis shows that the potato itself is made up of less than 2% total fat. Excessive usage of fatty oils in some versions of the french fry and chips plus too much slathering of butter, cream, and salt with other potato modes has tarnished the dietetic purity of this virgin vegetable. Bad potato preparation is not unlike giving a beautifully endowed maiden a bath in mascara and applying oversized uplifts. The potato is a package of protein, vitamins, minerals, and complex carbohydrates. Like a birthday present, it comes in a beautiful wrapper. But, unlike gift wrappings the potato's enclosure is a wholesome food. The potato's skin is not only good for you but it is good for the potato. It assures the contents an excellent shelf life.

The baked potato has always been a crowd pleaser. It is easy to prepare and easy to hold on the back of the stove for the late eater. A healthy alternative to the usual sour cream, butter topping is to try plain nonfat yogurt or low-fat cottage cheese blended with chopped scallions or chives. If you seek further choice, do your dabbing with a spoonful from a can of condensed asparagus or celery soup.

The twice baked version is a way of getting the cook to do the complete baked potato preparatory work.

Twice Baked In 6 Varieties

*B*ake washed POTATOES in a preheated oven at 450°F until done (about 40 minutes for small potatoes and 1 hour for large).

Cool until they can be handled, cut in half, lengthwise.

~Twice Baked In 6 Varieties~

Scoop out the pulp using care to keep skin in one piece.

Mix the pulp with your choice of one or more of the following:

(PLEASE, NO MORE THAN 2; WELL MAYBE 3)
1 tablespoon MILK per potato (dieters use SKIM)
1 tablespoon BUTTER per potato
(dieters use tub OLEO)
1 tablespoon shredded CHEESE
(like CHEDDAR)
1 tablespoon condensed SHRIMP SOUP
1 tablespoon condensed BROCCOLI SOUP
1 tablespoon mashed, cooked SALMON
(canned will be fine)
2 tablespoons freshly cooked and diced SCALLOPS
2 tablespoons cooked and shredded COD FISH

*R*eplace the enhanced potato pulp in the skin, dust the top with paprika and return to the oven with a lowered heat setting of 350° F for about twenty minutes.

If you have been using potatoes from Prince Edward Island, or Maine, and you have selected chopped scallops or shredded cod from the recipe choices you are hereby authorized to call your creation **DOWN EAST POTATO BOATS.**

With the potato's skin available, the eater gets an opportunity to ingest some natural potassium, fiber, iron, and other essentials to a good diet. Some food purveyors have tried to market the skins alone as an appetizer. Success has been only skin deep. It is distressing to learn that most of the jackets from baked potatoes are returned to the kitchen. Some people have trouble chewing them. If you are lying in this bed of thorns, salvation is just a few more paragraphs away in the mashed potato with edible skin.

THE MASHED, SMASHED POTATO

"Good mashed potatoes," Mark Twain observed, "do not occur everywhere." The art of mashing a potato is a skill that requires practice. The secret is smash them but don't knock the starch out of them. No less an authority than the ageless Fannie Farmer's epistle to the cook has warned against using a food processor. Pummeling cooked potatoes is much like painting a picture. There is a point where the potato, like the artist's canvas, has had enough. It was customary in the days of the Italian Renaissance for an art sponsor to hire an artist to paint a picture. Then the sponsor would hire a hit man to take out the artist before he spoiled the painting with excessive dabbing. So far, cooks have been more fortunate.

Now, to the matter of taming the potato peels in a tasteful, pleasing manner: Start with an Idaho "baking" potato, their jackets are potassium packed. Drop one uncut (skin on) potato per person into boiling water. This procedure reduces the loss of the C vitamin. Add

some onion or herbs for flavoring. In Turku, Finland, it is common practice to add a generous amount of dill weed to the boiling pot. A bit later in the boiling time, when the potatoes can be easily pierced with a knife, or the tines of a fork, drain the water and peel off the skins. Place the skins in a blender, add one slice of onion plus four salad croutons per potato and whirl away; having something in the blender besides potato skins helps the blade cutting action. Put the minced skins back in the pot with the potatoes. Add such other diary products and condiments as befits your temptations; a bit of butter and a modicum of milk, just enough milk to make the mixture "soft" (skim milk works fine). Take an old fashioned potato masher and count the strokes; like golf, the fewer the better. Par is usually four or five strokes. Don't get too far above par.

At this point in the ceremony one of a variety of cooked, chopped vegetables, fish, or meat may be "stirred in" by the cook. Some eaters prefer to do the "potatoes and" at the dining table. After several generations of making gravy ponds and mountain lakes with our mashed potatoes, we should be adept at mashed potato additives. Grandpa always mixed a little sauerkraut with his mashies whenever they occurred together at the same meal. On several occasions he has also been warned, when mixing peas with mashed potatoes, not to refer to them as peed potatoes.

Here are nine variations on a mashed potato theme:

IF YOU WANT	WHAT YOU ADD
Scarlet O'Tater	Cooked chopped beets
Spudnips	Cooked yellow turnip
Baby Bunting	Baby food veggies like carrots
Squeaky Leeky	Cooked, chopped leeks
French Pomme de Terre avec Fromage	Your favorite soft cheese
Bavarian Kartoffel mit Kohl	Sauerkraut
Adam and Eve	Applesauce
San Antonio	Salsa; mild, medium, hot?
Mississippi Mashers	Pork gravy

If you want to explore a new taste world try mixing in a little well-cooked parsnip. An interestingly different flavor can also be achieved with a touch of anise.

Now that you have access to the nine-plus kinds of smashed potatoes, how about, on your own, going for the other ninety-nine?

DID YOU KNOW THAT DINOSAURS ATE POTATOES BUT SPIT OUT THE SKINS? THEN, YOU KNOW WHAT HAPPENED? JURASSIC PARK!

Chapter 10

Menu Jargon And
How To Understand Code Talkers

An English statesman with an aspersion for American idioms once said that England and America were separated by a common language. It is true that in the States we do not ask, "Where's the loo?" when we are looking for a restroom. A woman from Boston doesn't open her bonnet when she wants a quart of oil in the engine of her car.

While an English couple was visiting, we drove by a New England farmhouse which displayed the sign, *NIGHT CRAWLERS*.

"Aha !" said our Oldham friends espying the barn, "Bet that's a lively pub."

In the United States we are big enough and diverse enough to have our own stateside communication problems. This can be recognized when a down Mainer passes through the state of Georgia. According to most inhabitants of Augusta (Augusta, Maine, that is, not Augusta, Georgia) grit is something you "git" from your forbearers. Hollywood screen writers once provided us with a two hour explanation of this word in the form of John Wayne's movie classic, *TRUE GRIT*. Grit is the stuff that makes you a self-reliant survivor. If you use the plural form, grits, it means you have a lot of it. In the

place where General William Tecumseh Sherman took *GONE WITH THE WIND*, the plural form is actually the only form of a word meaning a kind of breakfast food derived from hominy. Northerners sometimes order it in the singular form, grit, to indicate they don't want very much of it. Eventually, the Northerners found out that grits, like pants, do not come in the singular form. Even a side order of this food is a considerable amount.

It must be stated in fairness to our Southern cousins that grits are not only good for your morning constitution but they are merciful on sore gums. Grits in Georgia, however, are like poi in Polynesia: it's what you put on them that makes the difference—butter, salt, pepper, or sauce for the gander if you allow geese at your table.

Down Mainers are not to be outdone when it comes to using menu jargon the understanding of which is not widespread. Two words come to mind that are for the most part unintelligible to residents of the United States who live below the 42nd parallel: numshedooles and scouse. Since the numshes are usually taken at breakfast time we will deal with this strange, Biddeford, Maine, menu item first. A visiting Bostonian once described the numshedoole as a crêpe doughnut without a hole.

NUMSHEDOOLES
Recipe from an "original" circa 1921:

4 cups white FLOUR
1 teaspoon BAKING SODA
1 good shake from the SALT shaker
2 teaspoons CREAM of TARTAR

horoughly mix the above and stir in enough milk (about 2 cups) to form a dough. Roll out on a floured board until it is about as thick as a your smallest finger. Using an emptied soup can cut out circular dough pieces and dust with flour.

Drop them, one at a time, into a pan of hot oil (much like doughnuts). The oil could be bear grease or drippings left over from a venison roast. When the dough has browned transfer the numshes to a second pan that contains boiling molasses to which a bit of sugar or honey has been added.

N UMSHEDOOLES

THAT YOU CAN MAKE WITHOUT BEAR GREASE

oast some WHITE BREAD very lightly. Remove all crusts and BUTTER the remaining "soft" toast. Place in microwave dish, cover with syrup, and try 20 second bursts, turning after each burst until steaming hot.

Scouse, pronounced *skous,* was standard fare for seamen who sailed "Down Maine" in the 19th century. In Bucksport, some senior citizens say this single syllable word is a contraction from lobscouse. If there are more than two Mainers in the discussion one will insist that it is lobscourse, with an *r*. Little wonder that a summer visitor from Manhattan when asked if he'd like lobscouse for lunch replied, "I like lobster any time." Point of fact, lobscouse, or lobscourse, or

scouse has nothing to do with lobster. Scouse was something that was put together in the galley of a sailing ship with whatever vegetables that would withstand a "before-there-was-refrigeration" voyage. This included cabbage, potatoes, onions, and the "unvegetable" salt pork.

From Abbe Miller's cookbook written at the end of the 19th century: Fry up "some" salt pork in a heavy iron pan; add "some" potatoes, cabbage, onion, and "some" water (since the water used was seawater and the pork salted, there was little need to add salt). Cook "down" until the scouse has thickened. The sailors of this era did not, on average, have good teeth; they quickly learned that they could soften their sea biscuits (hardtack) in this hot vegetable stew. Scouse is one way of getting vegetables into the diet.

$\mathscr{S}$ COUSE

Recipe circa late 20th century. Put in a

heavy pan, on low to medium heat — for each person:

---

1 cup BEEF or CHICKEN BROTH
1 cup chopped CABBAGE
1 cup diced POTATO
1/2 cup chopped ONION
SALT and PEPPER to your taste

Cook and stir until the vegetables are soft. Don't forget to dunk your crackers.

Cuisine Après Dentist

The first commandment of reading a menu in any language is:

IF YOU DON'T UNDERSTAND IT, ASK !

I have displayed a talented knack for getting into language trouble. Instead of asking questions, I astutely reason my way into a pickle. While driving in Mexico I saw a traffic sign, *ALTO*. I immediately dismissed the thought of a female church choir member standing at the side of the road. Instead, I proceeded directly to the idea that the sign was calling our attention to the elevation. Everyone knows that alto is short for altitude. We were probably thousands of feet above sea level. A polite but firm traffic officer explained to me that *ALTO* also means *STOP.*

Then there was the sign *CUIDADO ! LOS GATOS.* "No problem," I said. "We're coming to some kind of fancy gates." Fortunately, the wild cats were not very hungry that day.

If you haven't been to a particular bistro before, take a few minutes to compliment the waitress/waiter and then ask about the chef's specialty. The skill of a chef grows like the skill of a brain surgeon. The ones who do their specialty frequently are better than the ones who do their thing occasionally. A pilot who lands his airplane 12 times a week is easier on his passengers than a pilot who lands his airplane 12 times a year. Even when you think you know the menu, it is sometimes prudent to seek clarification with examples that you understand. The cook's ministrations of salt, pepper, chili and their derivatives require specific calibration procedures before ingesting. Many Thai, Asian Indian, Caribbean, and Mexican menus will say in plain English: Mild, Hot and Very Hot. Remember these adjectives are relative and we don't mean a relative like Sweet Rosy O'Grady. It could be a relative like the black sheep in Pancho Villa's family. Ask, "mild" as in a one glass of ice water per entree, or is it a for-real four-glass "mild"?

Near Alice Springs, Australia, in the outback, there is a wonderful little pit stop. The menu showed a small red heart alongside two of the entrees. "Ah," said Mr. Know-It-All, "those are low fat, low salt items." "Not by your billabong," said the waitress. "Those are the heart stimulants of the day."

Time will come (Restaurateurs take note) when a tooth symbol will be depicted alongside certain menu items. Be sure to ask, "Is it tooth friendly or tooth challenging?"

When the people in one country do not trust the people in another country, like when they are at war or when they are at peace, the politicians and the military use a code to talk among themselves. This gives the code talkers a secure feeling. It also creates employment in the other country. The other country sets up a contingent of decoding technicians who try to figure out what the people in the first country are talking about.

In WW I General Pershing, of the U.S. Expeditionary Forces, was hard-pressed to devise a code that was unbreakable. One day his staff came up with a brilliant ploy: employ American Indians using their native tongue in the communication link. Putting one Navajo on the field telephone at the battle line and another one in the staff headquarters, every detail of strategy passed back and forth without the enemy understanding a single word; until a forward position was

overrun and a Navajo communicator captured. A day of grueling interrogation followed in which the enemy commander determined that if he could just get the Navajo to tell him the sense of a particular five-word communique, he would understand Pershing's battle plan. On the second day the Navajo decided to play the game. "AH," erupted the jubilant interrogator. "What do those five words mean?"

The Navajo translated: "Put more potatoes in soup."

**RHETT BUTLER TO SCARLET O'HARA,
"I DON'T CARE IF YOU ARE A SOUTHERN BELLE
ABOUT TO PEAL, IT'S YOUR GRITS I'M AFTER."**

Chapter 11

Teething By George Washington or Chewing Over Dental History

George Washington faced each national crisis with a tight face, a pinched lip, and a toothache. He had lost most of his natural teeth while he was busy soldiering in the French and Indian War. After that his time was pretty well taken up with running the American Revolution and becoming the first president. He had no time for dental office dallying so he devised a plan to handle his teeth maintenance which was quite revolutionary in its day. He invented teeth-by-mail. He kept up a barrage of letters and parcel post requests to his dentist. We are fortunate in this respect because much of Washington's dental correspondence has been carefully preserved allowing us to read the unexpurgated descriptions of the molar maintenance being employed during the 18th century. From the archives of the South Meeting House in Boston, Massachusetts, here is a sampling from a letter by G. Washington to his dentist, J. Greenwood, dated December 7, 1798.

Sir,

Your letter of the 8th came safe and as I am in a hurry in order to leave this city tomorrow, I must be short.

...I send the old bars [dentures], which you have returned to me with the new set...but they [the old set] may be destroyed, or anything else done with them you please, for you will find that I have been oblidged to file them away so much above, to remedy the evil I have been complaining of as

to render them useless...I feel much obliged by your extreme willingness, and readiness to accommodate me, and that I am, Sir.

Your Obedt Servant

Go. Washington

The Philadelphia Historical Society has a letter from Dentist Greenwood to Washington dated December 28, 1798.

Sir,

I send you enclosed two setts of teeth, one fixed on the Old Barrs [dentures] in part and the sett you sent me from Philadelphia which when I received was very black. Ocationed either by your soaking them in port wine, or by your drinking it. Port wine being sower takes of all the polish, and all acids has a tendency to soften every kind of teeth and bone...I have found another and better way of using the sealing wax when holes is eaten in the teeth by acids—first observe and dry the teeth, then take a piece of wax and cut it into small pieces as you think will fill the hole, then, take a large nail or any other piece of iron and heat it hot into the fier. Then put your piece of wax into the hole and melt it by means of introducing the point of the nail to it. I have tried it and found it to consolidate and do better than the other way and if done proper it will resist saliva. It will be handyer for you to take hold of the nail with small plyers. [YOU CAN BET YOUR BLISTERED GRABBERS THAT TAKING HOLD OF THE RED HOT NAIL WITH SMALL PLYERS WILL BE HANDYER] Sir, After hoping you will not be obliged to be troubled very sune in the same way, I subscribe myselvth your humble servant,

John Greenwood
PS Sir, The additonal charge is fifteen dollars...

Yes, during the 18th century tooth maintenance was a very crude affair and there were a lot of sore gums. Eating habits favored entrees like no-teeth-needed marrowbone stew and soft desserts like Indian Pudding. A generous quaffing of wine and rum helped the food go down.

. . . .

Marrowbone is a bone containing an edible, soft, vascular tissue of the animal. It is a major site of blood cell production and has at various times been highly regarded for its therapeutic value. In the historical novel, *Northwest Passage,* by Kenneth Roberts, a dramatic story relates the survival of the "Rangers" in the wilderness by existing on a concoction of marrowbone stew.

UPDATED VERSION OF ROBERTS' MARROWBONE STEW:

The preparation begins with a visit to the meat department of your favorite supermarket. Tell the meat cutter that you would like a few of the large beef bones sawed and cracked so that the center portion, or marrow, is exposed. Put the bones in a soup kettle, cover with water and set the stove for a low simmer. Add one bay leaf and one shake of salt for every soup bowl of water that you happen to be using.

Now comes the easy part: Cover the pot and simmer for about three hours while you attack the book that you have been going to read for the last three months, a fictional book like *How to Stay Married* by Elizabeth Taylor or *How to Build a Bridge to the Twenty-first Century* by Any Politician. Caution: Do not become so engrossed in your literary pursuits that you allow the water to boil away. Add liquid as necessary; keep the top on the kettle, and keep the simmer slow. If it makes you feel better poke the bone bits around with a wooden spoon now and then. Almost anytime toward the end of the third hour, turn off the heat and let the "soup" cool. Remove the bones and bone bits with a slotted spoon. Now at this point, if you were John Alden back at the Plymouth Plantation in 1620, this is the time that Priscilla would tell you to put the soup kettle outside on the back porch. Cover it over so the wild animals can't partake of it, and let the New England winter freeze the mixture. Did I forget to tell you to start this soup in January or February in the northern climates and July or August in the southern hemisphere? The freezing action forms a distillate layer of fat on the surface so that next morning, like John Alden, you simply lift this thin solid layer of the unwanted fatty part and toss it out.

If your wife's name is not Priscilla and since you may have started this recipe in April you can accomplish the same objective, distillation of the marrow soup stock, by transferring your soup pot contents at the end of the cooking/cooling period to the freezer compartment of the fridge. After a "gelling" period, discard the surfaced fat. This is a helpful procedure in the preparation of any soup or stew in which you want to get rid of excess fat.

With the essence of the distilled marrow in hand you can now proceed to complete this dish by adding chopped vegetables like cabbage, turnip, carrots, onion. Bring to a simmer and add seasoning to taste like pepper, oregano, bay leaf, and parsley. Cook until your tooth requirements are met, i.e., short time for crunchy vegetables or longer if you want them soft. Some cooks like to add a small can of tomatoes or tomato sauce. If the liquid appears to be running short add a few cups of water.

Separating unwanted fat from a liquid by freezing is akin to the old Yankee wintertime trick of making "Back-Stoop Applejack" by allowing fermented cider to freeze and skimming off the ice. After several days of this distillation process the saved part of the cider takes on considerable authority and has been favorably compared with "Kentucky White Lightning" and "Irish Poteen."

Indian Pudding was a favorite way of finishing an American colonial meal. The original is attributable to a joint effort of the Indians supplying the corn meal and the colonists contributing some molasses. Updating the recipe for Indian Pudding to our times goes like this:

*I*NDIAN PUDDING

TWO SERVINGS:

Combine in the top section of a double boiler:

1 pint MILK

1 tablespoon BUTTER (or OLEO)

1/8 teaspoon SALT

Keep the water boiling in the lower section until the contents of the upper section are thoroughly heated. Then, stir in:

1/4 cup CORNMEAL

Cook until the mixture starts to thicken (about 20 minutes)

Add and stir:

1 well-beaten EGG

1/3 cup MOLASSES

1/4 teaspoon CINNAMON

*I*NDIAN PUDDING

---

*P*our mixture into an ovenproof, 32 oz., baking dish and place in a preheated oven 350° F for about 60 minutes.

Pilgrim mothers served it hot, with a prayer. If you choose to put a scoop of vanilla ice cream on yours you can say a prayer too; be thankful that, unlike the Pilgrims, you not only have access to ice cream, you can choose from several flavors. Just let the hot pudding melt the ice cream until the whole dessert becomes a warm, tooth-friendly temperature.

It is often assumed that prehistoric people had good teeth. How else could they have shredded a mastodon steak? Maurice Smith in *A Short History of Dentistry* reports that out of a group of thirty-two human skulls found to be dating back to the Bronze Age, seven showed defective teeth. Modern forensic studies on the mummy of Ramses the Great, otherwise cataloged as Ramses II, showed that he suffered terrible teeth.

Evidence further shows that the need for cleaning one's natural teeth has been recognized since earliest times. The sponge technique used in the American colonial days proved to be as effective as throwing in a wet towel. The use of wooden sticks and scrapers was a slight improvement but the lack of a corner drug store vending a good dentifrice was sorely missed by many teeth.

A serious facet shines through the time-dimmed records: If we cannot feel the pain we can sense the agonies of dentistry that exist-ed in past ages. The memorabilia draw a sharp contrast with the dental environment that we live in today. We know, unlike George Washington, that relief is just a dental couch away. Modern medicine displays many miracles and today's dentistry provides some of the most convincing examples. A tip of the hat to our healer, the dentist, and to the American Dental Association. Our sincere thanks from the bottom of our molars, real or implanted.

❐ **QUESTION:** *WHAT DID GEORGE WASHINGTON SAY WHEN HE SAW THE CHERRY TREE ?*

❐ **ANSWER:** *"OH, FOR A GOOD SET OF CHOPPERS!"*

Chapter 12

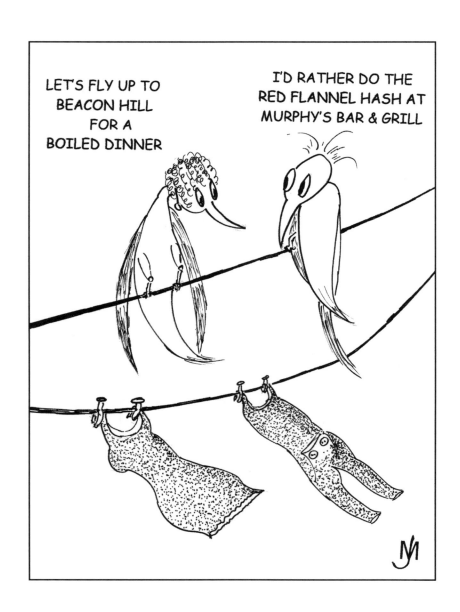

Hash, Stew, And Redos - Easy Tooth Foods

For over 200 years Boston has imported tea, rum and Irishmen. Another fortuitous event took place within the same time span. The Irish women came to America. The colleens of Cork and the maids of Mayo brought with them their grace, their charm, and the intimate knowledge that the way to a man's inner workings was through his taste buds. Specifically, they brought what was caricatured in the earlier days of the American comic strip, *Bringing Up Father,* corned beef and cabbage.

IRISH CORNED BEEF & CABBAGE

AS PRACTICED FROM DONEGAL TO CORK, FAMILY SIZED:

4 pounds (more or less) lean CORNED BEEF

4 peeled ONIONS

1 teaspoon THYME

1 tablespoon chopped PARSLEY

2 large CARROTS, cut up

4 CLOVES

2 pounds CABBAGE cut up in chunks

Cuisine Après Dentist

$\mathcal{P}$ lace beef in a heavy soup pot and cover with water. Insert a clove in each onion and add to the pot along with all other ingredients except the cabbage. Simmer slowly for three hours with a loose-fitting cover on the pot. This will allow the aroma to circumnavigate the building and make a house smell like a home. Add the cabbage and continue to cook until it is tender enough for your liking. Add pepper to taste. Be sure to have within easy reach on the dining table a cruet of malt vinegar and a jar of strong mustard. In Boston's Beacon Hill quarter the locals, or the we-were-here-first crowd, adopted this meat and cabbage union as The New England Boiled Dinner. However, as often happens in recipe relocations, the Boston version added several locally grown vegetables; one was an ivy league graduate, the Harvard beet. This subterranean, PhD'ed tuber added not only a touch of sweetness but gave this drab dish a dash of crimson.

When a New England Boiled Dinner, nee Corned Beef and Cabbage, is prepared in a traditional Boston environ one condition ensues: The quantity prepared is magnum cum voluminous. This leads to a surplus of NEBD lasting for several days. Because most New Englanders are both genetically generous and foodstuff frugal, it follows that the leftovers will be reprocessed. When properly done, this second-time-around can result in a tasty, few-teeth-required, Red Flannel Hash. The Harvard beets have by this time exuded enough red coloring to suggest the winter time undergarment.

RED FLANNEL HASH

HERE'S HOW ON A PER PERSON BASIS:

Finely chop and mix the following:

1/4 cup cooked CORNED BEEF

1/2 cup cooked CABBAGE

1 cooked, peeled POTATO

1 tablespoon chopped ONION or SCALLION

1/4 cup cooked BEETS

1 tablespoon MILK or BEEF BROTH

---

*H*eat a heavy skillet and add enough cooking oil to lightly coat the bottom. Add the chopped ingredients and slowly sprinkle on the milk or beef broth. Cook slowly over a low heat so that a tooth challenging crust does not form. Turn over and add more milk or broth to maintain the soft, tooth- friendly character.

There was a Boston mayor whose ancestral lines were sired in County Galway. His favorite meal was a C B & C dinner, the Irish way, like mother did it, no beets at all. The local, Faneuil Hall environmentalists, sometimes referred to as the double B's (Boston Brahmins), had enlarged his taste repertoire to the extent that he developed a liking for the next-day Red Flannel Hash. He sat one night in his favorite pub and before ordering the usual Jameson's Whiskey with a side order of corned beef and . . . he turned to his wife and asked: "Mary, do we have any beets in the pantry at home? If we do, I'll be taking along an extra portion of the beef and cabbage. Tomorrow you can be putting up some red flannel." Mary, Nee

Hurlihy, a thoroughbred at the subtle nuances of Irish humor replied: "No, James, I'll not be having your underwear washed 'til Monday."

Some food preparers have become so proficient in their procurement that many dining tables seldom show leftovers. When you finish a TV dinner, anything left over, besides the plastic tray, is not usually a good candidate for being reincarnated into edibility. Still, there were those Thanksgiving dinners when grand-père wanted to be sure there was plenty for everybody. There were those Sunday dinners when Uncle Tim and his two cousins didn't show. There were the lobster bakes and the fish fries and when the meal was finished it looked like the biblical miracle of the loaves and fishes. Everybody had stuffed, but still, the leftovers extended for three munching days. A thankful bow and a clap of the hands to the women and to the men who created from this overstock those remassaged dishes that not only taste good but, more importantly, work well with unwell teeth. Food like: après Thanksgiving turkey croquettes, or real English bubble and squeak, or fish stew, or fish chowdered patties.

An alternate route for acquiring the redo ingredients exists in the current practice of eating out. Like the Boston mayor, many diners patronize restaurants whose generous portions exceed their modest appetite. As one foresighted diner said to the waiter, "I'll have the king-sized roast beef and a doggie bag because I have the greatest recipe for meatloaf." Statistics from unknown sources show that many people who order doggie bags have no registered canines.

Many sophists and a few obituary writers peg tooth inconveniences as a problem limited mostly to teething infants and senior citizens. The science of orthodontics has developed around the teenaged customer. When grand-mère faced a teenager who said, "I'd rather die than be seen with those tooth straighteners," she said, "If you think growing up is tough, wait 'til you try growing old."

In dental dialect this translates: "If you think braces are bad, wait 'til you get to bridges." But that's another overpass to cross when you get to it.

Most teenagers heeded grand-mère's advice, kept their braces, and grew better teeth. The reason was not so much the persuasion of dental logic as the lure of her cooking. One of her popular dishes was Hot Dog Hash which she served along with her advice. This recipe has appeal to both oldster and youngster whose commonality is a tooth problem. On Saturday nights or Sunday evenings there is nothing more appropriate than this tube-steak supper.

Hot Dog Hash

FOR 2 PERSONS (readily expanded for a crowd):
1 cup cooked CORN (7 oz. can)
1 cup cooked BEANS (8 oz. can beans in tomato sauce)
2 tablespoons SALSA (mild, medium, hot — your choice)
2 finely chopped skinless FRANKFURTERS

Stir the above components together in a microwave dish and heat thoroughly.

Foodstuff, like golf, can be rated in a handicap system. When my sister and I were growing up, supper time was an enchanting hour. Occasionally, Mom would sneak in a quick can of Chef Boy-ar-Dee spaghetti, particularly, when she had a day crammed with teaching school, playing church organ, solving kid problems, and keeping the house spotless. My sister and I devised a rating system for our meals that was based on what we called The Chef Boy-ar-Dee A to Z taste score. If Mom served up a four-star topper like onioned hamburgers with no restrictions on the catsup, we would call it a Chef Boyar A Plus. A so-so dinner of chicken parts and mixed vegetables would be a Chef Boyar C. The appearance of broccoli automatically scored a Chef Boyar Y. Chef Boyar Z was reserved for spinach, cooked or otherwise. When it was a leftover that we didn't like it was dubbed Chef Boyar XXX. A triple X was like an UGH to the third power.

These ratings were never announced out loud but remained tacit to my sister and myself, unless it was an A. Then we let Mom know about it clearly and continuously. With the passage of time we came to the realization that Mom had silently understood our scheme all along. But, in her profound wisdom, she knew that she could attain her goal if she pretended that we were the smarter ones. A wise person can play the role of the dummy but the roles cannot be reversed.

There was, however, one point in her reasoning about food that bothered me. She would say, "Eat your carrots. In China there are starving people who would love to have your carrots." I always would think, "How can I possibly get these carrots over to China where they are needed so badly and how will my eating carrots help the starving Chinese?"

HASH, STEW AND REDOS CAN BE LIKE A
SECOND MARRIAGE:
THEY SOMETIMES WORK BETTER
THE SECOND TIME AROUND.

Chapter 13

Topless Pies or Does Our Society Need An Upper Crust?

There are several variations on a theme that deals with the preparation for a solo wilderness trip into northern Canada. All versions agree on the necessity for packing the essential clothing, sustenance, and the ability to know which direction to point when you say to yourself: "I'm out of here." One wizened explorer was asked, "What kind of compass or satellite tracker do you take along to find your way?"

The sage of the wilderness replied: "Never bother with such stuff. I just carry some cocktail makings in my backpack. If I get lost, I stop to make myself a martini. Some know-it-all will instantly appear from nowhere and tell me how much vermouth to use and where to go if I don't agree."

A parallel situation ensues when two or more Canadian Québécois fall into a discussion on the preparation of Pork Pie. One will insist on the addition of cloves or a pinch of poultry seasoning. A volley of exploding expletives follow: "Cloves? Mon Dieu! Your mother must have left you out too long on the Moncton tidal flats." But, in point of fact, from Trois-Rivieres to Ste Anne-de-Beaupré, I have never met a pork pie I didn't like.

In order to minimize further defections from Ottawa by the separatists, the preparation of the pork pie described herein permits a passel of provincial permissiveness. Factually, several liberties will be taken to improve the lot of those whose teething abilities are sub-Olympic.

Moses did not sculpt in stone, *THOU SHALT USE A PIE CRUST ON TOP OF EVERY PIE THAT THOU MAKEST.* Just because you have mastered the art of getting a super-market piecrust through the bag boy's crushing machine without a broken rim, you can still be party to promulgating a pork pie without an upper crust. *MAY THE GODS OF THE GASPE PENINSULA BE MERCIFUL FOR MY BLASPHEMY.* By doing this pastry topless, the sore-toothed hungry will be able to spoon it out of the bottom crust. They'll be able to mouth through this munchy meat treat like a lip-syncing, suede shoer at a like-Elvis twist off.

$\mathscr{P}$IQUANT $\mathscr{P}$ORK $\mathscr{P}$IE $\mathscr{S}$ANS $\mathscr{U}$PPER $\mathscr{C}$RUST

SUFFICIENT TO FEED 2 TEENAGERS or 6 ADULTS

1 9-inch PIE CRUST
2 tablespoons cooking OIL
1 large ONION, sliced thinly
1 pound ground BEEF
1 pound ground PORK
1 1/2 cup mashed POTATOES

1 teaspoon SALT
1/4 teaspoon PEPPER
1/2 teaspoon ground CLOVES
1/2 teaspoon POULTRY SEASONING

Seasoning: Feel free to implement or reject a particular item but as Madame DeFarge told her husband, "Try it my way first, then go ahead and do it your own way."

*H*eat oil and saute onion, beef, and pork. Drain any excess fat. Combine and thoroughly mix with the other ingredients and fill a 9-inch pie crust. Bake in a preheated oven at 375° F for 15 minutes. Then, sprinkle a tablespoon of water or beef broth onto the pie and lower the temperature to 325° F. Cook for an additional 25 minutes taking care to check that the top does not dry out.

Until I was twenty-nine years old I thought that kidney pies were something you ate to improve your renal functions, a sort of a dialysis diet. When I finally found out the truth of the matter I felt that the broad side of my education had been too narrow. In many pubs of the United Kingdom the kidney pie or the sometimes steak and kidney pie is addressed in reverential tones. If you patronize such an establishment you will find solace and sustenance in this tradition of ordinary, folk-food fare. Since the traditional kidney pie sports an upper crust but no bottom layer of pastry we may call this a bared-bottom meat pie. It is particularly good on those damp, bone-chilling, rainy spring, fall, winter and five days of English summer—especially if you have a toothache.

RECIPE FOR STEAK AND KIDNEY PIE,

often pronounced as

"STIKE END KID-KNEES"

SUFFICIENT FOR 4 HUNGRY PERSONS OR 5 "MODERATES"

1 1/2 pounds GROUND BEEF

6 LAMB KIDNEYS, washed and diced

4 tablespoons FLOUR

1 teaspoon SALT

1/8 teaspoon CINNAMON

1/2 teaspoon GROUND GINGER

1 teaspoon DIJON MUSTARD

---

1 tablespoon WORCESTERSHIRE SAUCE
4 medium, peeled, sliced ONIONS
2 1/2 cups WATER
1 PIE CRUST, 9 inch, to be used for a "top hat"

---

*M*ix the flour, salt, cinnamon, and ginger. Then combine with the meat. Coat the bottom of a skillet with a thin film of oil and saute the meat mixture. Add the remaining ingredients, stir, cover, and simmer for 1 hour. It may be necessary to adjust the water now and then so as to end up with a moist but not a soggy mixture.

Pour into a 9-inch Pyrex pie plate. Dampen the edge of the glass outer rim and cover with the pie crust. Using your thumbs, squeeze down the pie crust onto the glass. Some people prefer to do this sealing action with a fork. Punch a few holes in the crust with the tines of a fork so that the steam can sneak out without blowing its cover. Bake in a preheated oven at 425° F for 40 minutes.

The tasting of meat pies would be incomplete without sampling a shepherd's pie. Herein, for the touchy tooth person, is a for-real no-crust pie that's soft and warm all over. You can start with: "What kind of meat would you like, beef, chicken, pork, buffalo, or lest we lapse our shepherding, lamb?" Replace the baked pie dough cover with a paprika-dusted topping of mashed potatoes. The innards can be as healthy as a low-fat ground beef with softened kernel corn, festive bits of sweet red pepper, and tender onions.

Cuisine Après Dentist

~BASIC RECIPE~
for
SHEPHERD'S PIE

4 SERVINGS:

3 cups MASHED POTATOES (about 4 medium potatoes)
3 cups GROUND LEAN LAMB or BEEF or CHICKEN or PORK or
BUFFALO
1 medium ONION, minced
1 GARLIC CLOVE, peeled and diced fine
1 tablespoon sweet RED PEPPER, diced in small pieces
1 can (7 oz.) whole kernel sweet CORN
1/2 cup BEEF or CHICKEN BROTH
SEASONING: SALT and PEPPER to taste and
1 teaspoon ROSEMARY (if lamb is used)
1 teaspoon SAVORY (if beef or buffalo is used)
1/2 teaspoon POULTRY SEASONING (if chicken is used)
1 teaspoon BASIL (if pork is used)

---

*P*reheat a skillet with a little oil and saute the meat, onion, and garlic until the meat starts to brown. Add the corn, sweet pepper, mix well and cook for an additional 5 minutes. Transfer the contents of the skillet to a deep Pyrex pie dish, or 1 1/2-quart baking dish. Pour about 1/2 cup of beef broth over the ground meat, if beef, lamb or pork; chicken broth, if chicken. Stir in the appropriate seasoning as suggested in the recipe. Spread the mashed potatoes on top of the mixture using a spatula or wide knife.

Employ your best artistic stroking so that the potato covers the meat like a blanket. Bake in a preheated oven at 375° F for 30 minutes. Do not allow the potatoes to brown too much. When finished, dust the top with paprika and share this dish with your favorite sheep herder.

If the lower crust is omitted from a topless pie the result may be recognized by the short name, casserole, or the longer name, covered-dish-for-the-annual-church-supper-and-volunteer-fire-department-benefit.

Casseroles are a combination of complementing components, one of which is usually onion. One chef explained to me that the discrete addition of onion would improve just about any food mixture except, perhaps, ice cream. Some of my grandchildren believe that this chef is too restrictive in his use of the onion.

SQUASH CASSEROLE WITH ONION

FOR 6 SERVINGS YOU NEED:

1/2 cup coarsely chopped ONION
2 pounds yellow SUMMER SQUASH peeled and sliced
1 can (10 3/4 oz.) condensed CREAM of CHICKEN SOUP
1 cup SOUR CREAM
1 cup shredded CARROT
1 package (8 oz.) TURKEY STUFFING MIX
1/2 cup melted BUTTER or MARGARINE

Cook the onion and squash in boiling water for 5 minutes and drain. Mix the undiluted condensed chicken soup, sour cream, and carrots. Add the cooked squash/onion. Salt and

pepper to taste. Separately mix the melted butter and the stuffing and spread about half of the mixture in a 2-quart baking dish. Add the squash/soup mixture as a second layer. Sprinkle the remaining stuffing on top of the vegetables and bake in a preheated 350° F oven for 30 minutes.

Here is a casserole that started in the Colonial days of New Jersey, moved west with the pioneers to Indiana, and went on to meld with the Spanish culture in Arizona. Regional improvisations occurred in each geographical area.

THE JERSEY, INDIANA, ARIZONA BEAN-BAKE

FOR 6 SERVINGS YOU NEED:

1 large ONION, chopped

1 GARLIC clove, mashed and minced

1 pound ground PORK or BEEF SAUSAGE

1 (16 oz.) can PORK and BEANS, or BEANS in TOMATO SAUCE

1 (16 oz.) can LIMA BEANS (or 1 package of frozen LIMA BEANS prepared in accordance with instructions on package)

1 tablespoon LEMON JUICE

1 tablespoon BROWN SUGAR

1 tablespoon PREPARED MUSTARD (like it comes in a jar)

2 tablespoons SALSA (mild, or medium, or hot; your responsibility)

Mix thoroughly all of the above ingredients and pour into a baking dish. Cook for about 60 minutes at 375° F. Sausage links or patties may be used instead of ground meat if your teething abilities permit.

SIMPLE SIMON MET A PIE MAN

(As translated by a survivor of the Spanish Armada en route to a bake sale at Nottingham, England.)

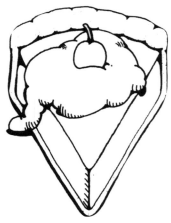

Señor Simon met a pie man,
peddling pastry for pay.
Simon was drooling,
for the pies that were cooling,
on this beautiful summery day.
Said Simon to pie man,
"I'm sighing, near dying,
to taste your pies. What say?"
Said pie man to Simon,
"Quit eyeing my pieing,
No pay, No way, Jose."

SOME YEARS LATER SEÑOR SIMON BOUGHT OUT MISTER PIEMAN.
IT'S NOW CALLED *Sigh's Pies To Go* !

Chapter 14

Doable Turkey
And Viable Veal

The day before a holiday can hold as much excitement as the fete day itself. Our inner mind nibbles on tidbits of anticipation. The day before Thanksgiving in New England can be a kaleidoscope of expectations; not that this Pilgrim holiday doesn't run for a full 24 hours in every other region of the country. In the northeast corner, however, the fall air has now become crisper. Yellow pumpkins pose on doorsteps and crunchy apples wait at farm stands. The spired steeples seem whiter against a bright blue sky. Everyone walks a little faster, smiles a little more, and talks. Almost everyone talks; there are some who sit silently, and wait, and worry.

Timothy Weatherbean tried to watch the TV, but his bundled thoughts were on tomorrow, Thanksgiving. He was spending full time worrying whether his daughter would come for him, would he be able to eat, would he make it through the day without losing his patience or his continence.

Being Tim Weatherbean's daughter was also a full-time occupation. Besides mothering two children, housing a husband, and writing software for that Cambridge outfit, she too was anticipating the holiday. Tomorrow's time would be divided up like the traditional pumpkin pie: a piece to the intercity football rivalry, a piece to the family dinner, a special piece to each member of the family, and Pops with that pesky tooth problem just at holiday time.

Wednesday became Thursday and Thursday became get-the-meal-ready time. As the roasted turkey was nearing the-moment-of-truth she had a flashback to a Thanksgiving past, a day of memories for a young lady, a day when one of her wisdom teeth was not showing any intelligence. It was sore, very sore. Mom had made things better with a last minute food-fixing. Tim Weatherbean's daughter fought the nostalgia by marshaling the troops into action. "Jack, get the silverware and napkins." "Joey! Fill up everybody's water glass." "Pops, you sit there at the head place. Wait 'til you see what we have for you." "Honey, the turkey is cool enough to cut. Do your carving act." She watched the juicy turkey slices accumulating on the large platter. Then, she deftly transferred one into the food processor, switched on, switched off, removed the finely minced meat, stirred in some of the gravy and mounded it on a plate in an attractive pyramid. In another sweeping motion she added a spoonful of the soft oyster dressing and some cinnamon mashed sweet potatoes. The presentation to Pops was without ceremony but with a casual remark: "Pops, I know how you like your turkey a little softer." Pops was thankful. It was going to be a good day.

With turkey available year-round you don't have to wait until Thanksgiving for tooth-friendly doable turkey.

🦷

⬧ᴇIGHT 𝒮OFT 𝒯URKEY 𝒞ROQUETTES⬧

2 cups cooked and cut up TURKEY PIECES
1 small ONION, peeled
5 or 6 fresh stalks of PARSLEY
8 SALTINE CRACKERS
1 can condensed CELERY SOUP
1 EGG, beaten lightly
2 teaspoons LEMON JUICE
1 tablespoon WATER or MILK
PEPPER to taste
Pinch ground CELERY SEED
Pinch NUTMEG
PEANUT OIL for cooking

*P*lace the turkey, onion, parsley, and crackers in a food processor or blender and chop. Transfer to mixing bowl and add 1/2 can of the celery soup, egg, lemon juice, and pepper. Mix thoroughly. After chilling the mixture in the fridge for about 20 minutes, form into cones with your hands. Think about the shape of those orange, traffic cones that are put on the highways when they repaint the white lines. If you manage to get eight croquettes, they will be the right size to cook through without having to be crusty on the outside. On the back burner, set to low heat, place the rest of the celery soup in a small pan together with a tablespoon of water or milk, a pinch of ground celery seed, and a pinch of nutmeg. Stir occasionally.

Heat oil in a deep skillet or french frier to 360° F. Test the temperature by dropping in a freshly cut piece of bread, about the size of one of your croquettes. If it browns readily, the oil is the correct temperature. Cook the croquettes a few at a time so that you can keep them rolling around and not become crusty. Remove and drain on a paper towel. Keep warm in a toaster oven until all of the croquettes are finished. Serve with a few spoonfuls of the back burner, thick celery soup. Peas make a nice traveling companion to the turkey croquettes.

If you want to time-travel in medieval England without giving up 21st century creature comforts, walk through the gates of the fortress town of Chester. A massive stone wall encircles the old city, and 26 scattered towers stand as silent sentries. Located some 175 miles from London's Piccadilly Square on the estuary of the river Dee, Chester comes complete with a high sheriff, a lord mayor, and a cathedral. Afternoon tea is served in the Grosvenor Hotel on Eastgate Street. Travelers from the former colonies are permitted to discretely dunk their scones while reflecting on how close their homeland came to being a part of the British Empire. The dinnertime food includes ample choice of fish and fowl, fruit and fauna. The tooth-impaired will find solace in the English-style, softened, and well-cooked vegetables. Bubble and squeak, for one, is a well-chopped cabbage/sausage combo with a white sauce. Most of the sauces are excellent and have benefited, I suspect, from the proximity to France and the Gallic palate; it is tastefully evident that the English house wines have.

The restlessness of the American appetite is never more evident than when a Yankee dwells too long in the same venue. Succinctly stated: "Let's try Italian." In this aspect, the modern, the medieval, and the ancient Chester are not found lacking. We intone Saluto!

We hie ourselves off to a Ristorante for "pasta and." One of our party is complaining of a bite problem. The cameriere suggests the "Spechee-al-ah-tee" of the house, Veal Cacciatore. He insists that even sensitive teeth will be able to handle his veal. It is so tender he insists it can be cut with a dull fork. Our subsequent, denuded plates attest to our satisfaction with his recommendation. Even our sore tooth, eating companion is sated. We call for the manager. We call for the chef. We must include them personally along with the waiter in our chant: "The food—Magnificamente."

"To think, in the very heart of merry old England you can find such superb Italian food." The apron-clad, one person, manager-chef led us outside and pointed to an inscription on the massive stone wall. He read aloud, "Dedicated to the Emperor Hadrian who first camped here with his Roman legions in the first century A.D." He added, "You see, we Italians have been here a very long time."

VIABLE VEAL CACCIATORE
(you can cut it with a dull fork)

For 4 persons buy about 1 pound of center cut VEAL, or steak cut from the leg. There is usually very little fat on this cut. Have the veal ground at the market or start your preparation by fine chopping the meat in the food processor together with one peeled shallot and six "Caesar" salad croutons (substitution 2 scallions and 3 saltine crackers).

You will also need in the order of appearance:

1 EGG, beaten

1/4 cup MILK

1/4 teaspoon OREGANO

Pinch of SALT and pinch of PEPPER

1/2 tablespoon OLIVE OIL

1/2 tablespoon BUTTER

1 can (10 3/4 oz.) condensed TOMATO SOUP

2 tablespoons red WINE

2 tablespoons grated PARMESAN CHEESE

1 can (7 oz.) MUSHROOM pieces

1 teaspoon BASIL

1 can (16 oz.) prepared SPAGHETTI in tomato sauce

In a 2-quart bowl, mix together the chopped veal, egg, milk, oregano, salt and pepper. Using your hands make 4 flat patties. Over medium heat blend oil and butter. Brown the veal patties evenly on both sides, cooking about two or three minutes per side. Spoon the condensed soup into an 8x8x2-inch Pyrex, baking

dish, or equivalent. Spread it around evenly and place the patties gently into the tomato liquid. Anoint with wine. Sprinkle with Parmesan cheese. Spread mushroom pieces on top of the cheese evenly. Dash on the basil and top with the prepared can of spaghetti. Bake in a preheated oven 350° F for 40 minutes.

MY HEART BELONGS TO DADDY BUT
MY TUMMY IS COMPLETELY IN THE HANDS OF THE COOK.

Chapter 15

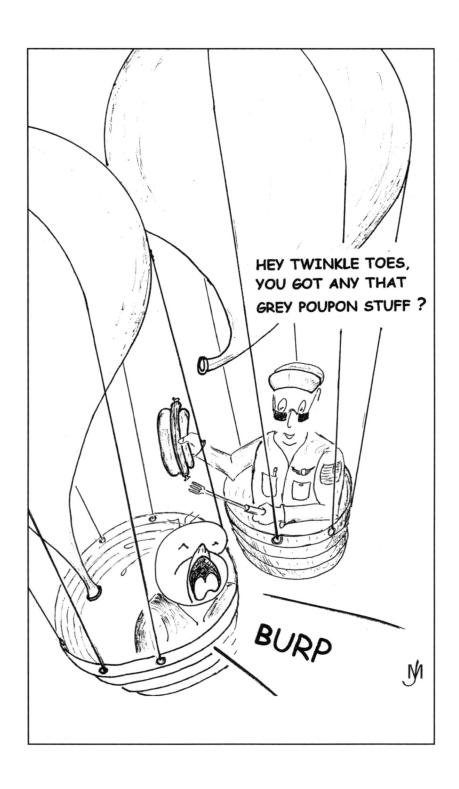

Pancakes With Ginger Ale
Or Light As A Balloon

If I were to design a favorite uncle I would build him with a great sense of humor and a truckload of compassion. He wouldn't have to be rich, he would just have to have time, time to spend with kids. One of my good fortunes was that I didn't have to manufacture a favorite uncle. I inherited one. Riding in his open "touring" car one day, we spotted a sign along the highway, FOOD-GAS. Uncle Melvin had one comment: "That sign could be a short title for a long story, first the eating then the gas."

He was always teaching me something that educators later discovered and now call the hands-on method. One day he took me for a balloon ride at the county fair. As we watched the balloon's bag being filled, he said, "Reminds me of the way I feel after the second piece of mincemeat pie."

I don't remember too much about the actual ride except that when the driver shut off the hot air generator it got real quiet. We could hear the people on the ground talking. There was another balloon floating near us and I suppose the inevitable had to happen. Someone in this other balloon called out to us: "Pardon me, but do you have any grey poupon?" I did learn a couple of things from that balloon ride: (1) Never drink two bottles of carbonated soda water just before you take off to new heights. (2) Never eat two frankfurters with beans, ditto. As you soar upward the air pressure outside your

personal envelope becomes lower than the air pressure inside your personal envelope. Some of the inside stuff is expanding. It wants to get with the outside stuff. One of the things that a parent fears when taking the kids out to dinner is a sudden pressure equalization, the unannounced burp. Physicists have enacted all sorts of laws about air pressure looking for a way out, but as my uncle stated it: "A pent up gas is like a hot air politician, it has to vent somewhere. Sometimes it burps in your town, sometimes it burps in Washington."

A couple of Frenchmen named Montgolfier worked out some of the early ballooning protocols. They both had the same name because, it seems, they were brothers. In addition to being inventors they were descendants of French aristocracy. The first proclivity led to designing balloons, the second to quaffing champagne. After several near disasters attributed to imbibing while flying (which caused their heads to soar higher than their balloon) they logged-in a set of flight rules which bade all "would be" astronauts to fly first and drink later.

The principle, a pent up gas will try to enlarge its holder, was applied to food preparation long before the science community wrote the gas laws. Swiss cheese holing and yeast bread rising are examples of letting a trapped and pushy gas expand and lighten the product.

~LIGHT AS A BALLOON PANCAKES~

On the next batch of Sunday morning pancakes, try substituting ginger ale for the milk or other designated liquid. Your nutritional conscience will dictate sugar free, or regular, but make it fresh and active ginger ale. Do not stir the pancake mixture any more than necessary to "wet" the flour. Let the pent-up carbonated gases expand

and, reduce the density of your griddle cakes. You can then chomp with the best of them because your breakfast will not only be easier to chew, it will be as light as a balloon.

❒ **QUESTION:** *WHAT IS THE DIFFERENCE BETWEEN IRISH PANCAKES AND FRENCH CREPES ?*
❑ **ANSWER:** *SAINT PATRICK FORGOT THE BRANDY.*

Chapter 16

Just Desserts or
How To Make A Great Finish
with A Finnish Flan

Fruit and fiber have been the consistent cry of many health-bent food regimens. Historical fact shows that food moguls have followed this trail of crumbs for centuries. Consider the behavior of the French monarch, Louis XIV, who suffered toothaches throughout his entire adult life. He was constantly seeking a soft shoulder or a no-teeth-needed dessert. In planning the third war of his multi-war reign, he sent the Marquis of Frangipani (that was his real name, pronounced, Fran-gee-pan-ee) to give some of France's land-grabbing rivals a comeupance.

One evening, following a hard day of romping around Holland fighting France's eternal foe, the English, the Marquis sat down to his dinner. Although he had a severe toothache at the time, he was a firm believer that it was better to eat some of the stew than to stew about some of the eats. Toward the end of this unsatisfactory repast, a young lady showed up at the sentry post with a basket of fruit compote. The practice of buttering up the invading army with food and other peace offerings was a perfected practice in the seventeenth century. Being blonde and winsome the young lady was permitted into the camp. The Marquis evaluated both the winsome girl and the winsome dessert. He judged the first to be a friendly honey and the

second to be a friendly flan — both tooth-friendly desserts. He post-poned all further battle engagements until he could fathom the recipe. Then, after thoroughly testing the concoction, he dispatched a messenger to carry the formula back to the Versailles kitchens of King Louie. The Marquis, also knowledgeable as to who was buttering his bread, cleverly titled the dish, Frangipani's Fruited Flan, a Dish Fit for The Greatest of French Kings. Scribes have not recorded the full impact of this flan on history. Nevertheless, it is interesting to trace three significant events that took place after the French "discovery" of this Dutch Treat: (1) Louis XIV promoted the Marquis de Frangipani to the rank of major general. (2) The Dutch-French Fruit Flan started to show up at London dinner parties. (3) The historic Treaty of Ryswick was signed in 1697. This agreement stopped the war with the provision that all participants hold their peace as well as their pieces of real estate.

As the noted history buff, Winston Churchill, who also experi-enced something less than perfect teeth, observed: "Let history show that a single good emerged from the wars between the fourteenth French Louis and our William of Orange. It was the Fruited Flan." Churchill was reported to have been particularly adept at snatching a flan from a passing dessert trolley.

Lest you conjure a misplaced sympathy for the winsome lady whose recipe was appropriated by the filching Frangipani, the worn threads of history hint that, in the early 1600s, a Dutch traveler picked up the whole package when he went ashore on strawberry festival day in Helsinki. The tributary title to this toothsome treat should therefore be: *A FRENCH FRANGIPANI, FINNISH FRUITED,*

FLEMISH FIBERED FLAN. In order to frugally parcel our time and space we will henceforth refer to this historically bandied brunch food as: *THE DESSERT OF THE SEVEN EFFS* or simply *FRANGI'S FLAN*.

There is an area in London between the Strand and Maiden Lane that contains the Savoy and Rules restaurants, both noted guardians and purveyors of the "original" flan. When prepared with a softened, multi-grained pastry crust this dessert represents the epitome of the tooth weary, fruit and fiber diet. Too bad that King Louie didn't know about these fruity desserts at an earlier age; he might have saved himself a war or two.

FRANGI'S FLAN

1 GRAHAM CRACKER 9-inch PIE SHELL
1/2 cup STRAWBERRY JAM (or PEACH PRESERVES)
3 cups cut up fresh STRAWBERRIES (or PEACHES),
save a bit of fruit for garnish
1 cup SUGAR
1/3 cup FLOUR
1/8 teaspoon SALT
2 EGGS, beaten
1/2 cup SOUR CREAM
1/2 cup FLOUR
1/4 cup BUTTER

Cover inside of pie crust evenly with strawberry jam and spread fresh strawberries on top of the jam. Combine the next three items in the recipe, the sugar, flour, and salt in a mixing bowl. Add the eggs and sour cream and stir until uniformly mixed. Pour this mixture over the strawberries. Work the last two items (butter and flour) together until a uniform, crumbly mixture results. Sprinkle this flour mixture on the top and bake at 350°F for 60 minutes. Use some fresh fruit for a topping when you serve this flan.

As wars pass there is mixing and melding of the surviving combatants and their progeny. Old confrontations reform into competitive economic, athletic, or gastronomic combat. With the American Civil War buried under a century plus of moldy history, we can still detect the rivalry, now friendly, where the thoroughbreds from the North meet the thoroughly bred from the South at the supper table.

The story of the bakeoffs between Key Lime "piers" and Shoo-Fly "cobblers" is a story of the Carolina confrontations. Many teeth-sensitive dessert lovers have identified these meetings as undisguised pie-eating contests. The informal spontaneity of these events can be more fully grasped by considering the background and circumstances which lead up to this fortuitous convergence.

Driven by primeval, migratory forces there is a certain time of year when some Floridians go North and then South, and some Pennsylvanians go South and then North. A particular segment of the southern strain starts from the various key locations, like: Key West, Key Largo, Cedar Key, Longboat Key, Siesta Key, Oyster Key, Chokoloskee, Conche Key, and Kissimmee, to name a few.

The Pennsylvania Dutch originate mostly from towns around Kutztown, like: Allentown, Pottstown, Brownstown, Elizabethtown, Quakertown, Norristown, Winterstown, and Stewartstown. One group from Philadelphia has been ruled out because it was later

determined that they were itinerants interested only in southern sun-bathing.

As the spring equinox approaches, the northerners are headed back home "up-North" and the southerners are headed down to reclaim their places in the sunny South. The twain meet in the trailer parks of the Carolinas. The azaleas are in bloom and a spirit of elan pervades. The trailer parks become covered with cooking odors in the evening very much like the way the dew covers Dixie in the morning. Getting asked over to the next encampment to exchange desserts is the peak of piquantness.

The "Keyers" have equipped themselves with their best Florida key limes. These limes are a little smaller than the California version but the Florida strain has a tad more zip because of higher acid content. The next time you run into your green grocer you can tax his trivia quotient by insisting on real Florida key limes. Don't be satisfied with the weak-pH, no-zip variety.

The Kutztown crowd came prepared by lardering in molasses, brown sugar, and shortening. Some of the purists from Strasburg, even though they are not in the official Pennsylvania Shoo-Fly town list, bring their own "from home sweetener" known as King syrup. The Strasburg crowd has also been known to add a few pinches of cinnamon.

Most full molar eaters believe that this flexing of baker's biceps usually ends in an even scoring of the pastry entrants. Some participants insist on overtime, as in some pro ball contests, a sudden death session, i.e., one more score for pies after eating a score of pies. Other saner sated folks whose stomachs have gone the distance say, "Let's do it again, but make it same time next year."

In this corner, from the Florida Keys, the famous:

KEY LIME PIE

❯·❯·❯·❯·❯·❯·❯

---

1 PIE SHELL, 9-inch

4 EGG yolks

6 EGG whites

1 can CONDENSED MILK

1/2 cup LIME JUICE

3/4 cup SUGAR

1/4 teaspoon CREAM of TARTAR

---

*B*eat egg yolks until lemon colored and slowly blend in with the condensed milk. Add lime juice and stir until thoroughly mixed.

In a separate bowl add cream of tartar to egg whites and beat until foamy. Add sugar, small bit at a time, while continuing to beat until egg whites peak to form the meringue.

Gradually work about 6 tablespoons of the white meringue into the egg yolk part of the mixture. Use a rubber spatula with a gentle caressing movement. Pour this into the pie shell. Cover evenly with the remaining meringue and bake in the middle shelf of an oven pre-heated to 350°F until the top browns.

In this corner from Shoo-town Pennsylvania:

THE SHOO FLY PIE

1 9-inch PIE CRUST
1 1/2 cups FLOUR
1/2 cup BROWN SUGAR
4 tablespoons BUTTER
3/4 cup boiling WATER
3/4 cup MOLASSES
1/2 teaspoon BAKING SODA

Mix the flour and the sugar. Cut up the butter and work it into the flour with your hands.

Stir the molasses into the hot water and add the baking soda. Pour the molasses mixture into a 9 inch unbaked pie shell and sprinkle the buttered/flour on top. Bake in a preheated oven, 375°F. It will take about 1/2 hour.

The tooth-handicapped should also ponder the plethora of pudding choices: rice, tapioca, bread, Indian, chocolate, orange, fig, corn, parsnip, pumpkin, lemon, rhubarb, plum, persimmon.

BAKED RICE PUDDING

THIS RECIPE IS LIKE A BIG BUICK: IT WILL TAKE CARE OF 6 PEOPLE

4 cups MILK
1/2 teaspoon SALT
SUGAR to taste, try 1/3 cup

2 tablespoons RAISINS (or CURRANTS)
1/2 teaspoon NUTMEG
1/2 teaspoon CINNAMON
3 tablespoons RICE (not instant)

*S*tir all ingredients in a buttered baking dish and place in a preheated oven, 300°F for 30 minutes. Without burning yourself, stir the hot mixture so as to distribute the rice evenly. Continue baking for an additional 60 minutes. Serve with a cream or non-dairy topping. Some like it hot, some like it cool.

If your button hasn't been pushed so far, think about sorbets, sherbets, sweet souffles, candied yams, yogurt and bananas — bananas like they serve in New Orleans:

BANANAS FOSTER

1 tablespoon BUTTER
2 tablespoons BROWN SUGAR
1 Ripe BANANA, peeled and sliced lengthwise
Dash CINNAMON
1/2 oz. BANANA LIQUEUR
1 oz. RUM
1 scoop VANILLA ICE CREAM

*M*elt butter in a skillet using low heat. Add sugar and banana stirring carefully with a spatula or wooden spoon. When heated sprinkle cinnamon, pour in the liqueur and rum and light with a match. When flame burns out serve this special banana over the ice cream. Have fire extinquisher at hand before starting this operation.

~DRAMBUIED (DREAMBOAT) YAMS~

FOR EACH PERSON YOU NEED:

1 medium SWEET POTATO
Some BUTTER, HONEY, BROWN SUGAR, and DRAMBUIE

Boil sweet potatoes until they can be easily penetrated with the tines of a fork; do not overcook. Cool, peel, and place in a baking dish. Spread 1 teaspoon of honey and 1/2 jigger of Drambuie on each potato. Sprinkle with a little brown sugar, place few dabs of butter on each potato and bake in a preheated oven at 350°F for twenty minutes.

Pour 1/2 jigger Drambuie on each potato and cook for additional 5 minutes. Cut each potato into thick slices and serve hot.

A perfect dietary day could begin with a fruit-juice-soaked fiber, breakfast food topped with fruit. The final meal of your day could end with a raisin, rice pudding. Since most fruits by themselves contain appreciable fiber this double-barreled fiber attack could help you win your long-range tooth battle and prepare, short term, the rest of your working parts to fight another day.

THREAT: YOU DON'T GET ANY DESSERT UNTIL YOU EAT ALL YOUR VEGETABLES.
RESPONSE: MAKE THE VEGETABLES DRAMBUIE YAMS AND FORGET DESSERT.

Chapter 17

Random Quotes
On Molars And Meals

After his return from the moon, astronaut Jim Lovell Jr., commander of Apollo 13, shared this "down-to-earth" food recipe with the members of the Explorers club in New York City.

$\mathscr{S}$HRIMP, $\mathscr{A}$VOCADO $\mathscr{S}$ALAD

FOR 6 to 8 EARTH PEOPLE, YOU NEED:

1/2 cup SALAD OIL

1/2 cup LIME or LEMON juice

2 tablespoons VINEGAR

1 1/2 teaspoons SALT

1 teaspoon DILL SEED

1 teaspoon DRY MUSTARD

Dash CAYENNE PEPPER

1 pound cooked SHRIMP, shelled and cleaned

4 AVOCADOS, halved and peeled

1 head BOSTON LETTUCE

*T*o make tooth-friendly, use very ripe avacado and dice both the avacado and the shrimp. Prepare the marinade by mixing the oil, lime juice, vinegar and seasonings. Marinate the shrimp and refrigerate until chilled. Arrange avocado pieces on shredded lettuce with shrimp and marinade.

Just one hundred and one years before the Apollo mission, another adventurer, searching for the "lost" David Livingston, made a discovery. Henry M. Stanley, an American newspaper reporter, "found" David Livingston, the missionary doctor, ministering to the needs of the citizens in central Africa. History recorded Stanley's greeting as, "Doctor Livingston, I presume." History is less certain about Livingston's reply. One version recalls that Livingston, who liked to fool around with cooking, replied: "Pull up a camp stool and have some of my Scotch broth."

Stanley sipped and said: "Wow! Doctor, you do like pepper."

Paul Harvey, another American media person, has made a career chasing down "the rest of the story." Suppose, for the moment, Paul Harvey was listening when the following historical sayings were first uttered:

Captain Lawrence during the battle of Lake Erie: "Don't give up the ship."

Would Harvey have commented ? "The rest of the story was — the cook can't swim."

General Tony McAuliffe's reply when asked to surrender at the Battle of the Bulge: **"NUTS!"**

Harvey: "What he really said was, 'I gotta stop cracking **NUTS**— with my teeth.'

Will Rogers: "I never met a man I didn't like."

Harvey: "Especially if he can cook."

Admiral Farragut at the battle of Mobile Bay, "Damn the torpedoes, full speed ahead!"

Harvey: "Hurry up! I gotta get to a dentist fast."

Arthur Sulzberger: "Freedom cannot be trifled with."

Harvey: "Neither can apple pie."

English Proverb: "The proof of the pudding is in the eating."

Harvey: "Especially Haggis and other Scotch puddings."

Christopher Morley: "A human being is an ingenious assembly of portable plumbing."

Harvey: "More like a computer-driven garbage disposal."

Persian Prophet: "The Lord who made thy teeth shall give thee bread."

Harvey: "And, if you lose your teeth pray for milk toast."

James Thurber: "It's a naive domestic Burgundy without any breeding, but I think you'll be amused by its presumption."

Harvey: "I've eaten food like that."

Robert Benchley: "I must get out of these wet clothes and into a dry Martini.

Harvey: "Amen."

Alexander Woolcott: "All the things that I like are either immoral, illegal, or fattening."

Harvey: "Then he added, 'After that last dentist visit I had one of each.'"

Julia Child, when chided for her liberal use of butter and cream in her recipes, replied: "We already have all those government regulations to worry about, now we've got Nutritional Police."

The late Barry Goldwater, retired air force general and former U.S. senator from Arizona, once said at one of his lectures: "To love Arizona you have to love the land and the cooking. About cooking, I have never considered myself anything but an old-fashioned cowboy-type cook. If it will fit into a fry pan, cook it, and the more variety of things in there with it the better." Maybe that's why he recommended his wife's recipe for campfire beans; they fit in a frying pan.

~ Campfire Beans ~

FOR 5 or 6 PEOPLE, YOU NEED:

2 pounds PINTO BEANS
2 large ONIONS
4 cloves GARLIC
2 teaspoons SALT
1/2 teaspoon BLACK PEPPER
1 can of TACO SAUCE
1/2 teaspoon CUMIN SEEDS
1 can ROASTED GREEN CHILIES
1 can TOMATOES

*S*oak pinto beans in cold water overnight. Drain, wash, and cover in about 2 inches of water. Add salt, and boil over moderate heat for about 1 hour, adding water as needed. Dice onion and garlic. Chop green chili. Mix the garlic, onion, and chili with the taco sauce and tomatoes. Stir this into the beans. Cook over reduced flame for 1 1/2 hours or until beans are tender. If spicier beans are desired, this may be achieved easily by the addition of 1 or 2 teaspoons of red chili powder."

One way to speed up the process is to start with canned pinto beans. These are already softened and very tooth-friendly. Mix all ingredients, heat thoroughly, and call the ranch hands.

Everyone should have some exposure to chili powder and horses. There are some, however, who will go to great lengths to avoid both confrontations. This evasion can contribute to a complete lack of understanding in these matters, as for instance, those people who believe that a bareback rider is a shirtless cowboy.

Thorton Wilder became so absorbed in the writing of the award winning play, *By The Skin of Our Teeth*, that he missed two dentist appointments.

ANONYMOUS said, "De gustibus non disputandum (There is no accounting for tastes)."

But, isn't it funny how everybody knows when it's bad."

ANONYMOUS also said:

"The way to get to be a mature film star is to out-live the rest of 'em, and oh yes, brush your teeth."

"Teeth and money are alike; fools get parted from both."

🖎 🖎 🖎 🖎

"A filling in time should have been done last month."

🖎 🖎 🖎 🖎

"I would have made it from scratch but I wasn't itching."

🖎 🖎 🖎 🖎

A 19th-century chemist once said, "Take 2 Adolf Wilhelm Hermann Kolbes and call me in the morning." No wonder the dentists wouldn't allow Kolbe, the inventor of aspirin, into the ADA.

🖎 🖎 🖎 🖎

Brushing after every meal is good tooth protocol but give your taste buds 10 minutes to enjoy themselves.

🖎 🖎 🖎 🖎

Too many sweets to Sweetie and Sweetie has to go to the dentist.

🖎 🖎 🖎 🖎

Diamonds may be a girl's best friend, but they're no substitute for a good set of teeth.

🖎 🖎 🖎 🖎

If you get your "teeth into it", keep your "shoulder to the wheel", and your "nose to the grindstone", you will not only need a dentist, you'll need a chiropractor, a plastic surgeon, and a sober psychiatrist.

SOME ANSWERS YOUR DENTIST NEVER TOLD YOU:

QUESTION: **What did Juliet say to Romeo?**
ANSWER: **"If I marry you, am I covered by your dental plan?"**

Q. **If an eye for an eye equals a tooth for a tooth, how many contact lenses equal a molar implant?**

A. **Consult: Allowable fees for optometrists/dentists, section 8, paragraph 23, Medicare guidelines.**

Q. **"Are tooth fairies real?"**
A. **"Yes, as long as Mom or Pop pays the dentist's bill."**

Q. **What's the difference between a stomachache and a toothache?**
A. **STOMACHACHE: Something didn't stop at the tooth station long enough to get chewed over.**
TOOTHACHE: Someone didn't stop at the dentist's office often enough to get flossed over.

~ *QUESTIONS PERTAINING TO FOOD* ~

QUESTION: **"Remember the Alamo?"**
ANSWER: **"Is that a fast-food place or a car rental?"**

Q. **John Wayne?**
A. **"What you turkeys need are some true grits."**

~ *UPDATING TOOTHY QUOTES* ~

☞From the *Old Farmer's Almanac,* "In youth the absence of pleasure is pain; in old age the absence of pain is pleasure."
UPDATING: "For some who are young, and some who are old, there is nothing but pain and pleasure; teething and eating."

☞From the Biblical text of John, Chapter 2, verses 1 -10: Scene, The Marriage at Cana:

The mother of Jesus said to him, "They have no wine. "

UPDATING: "And remember son, with fish always make it white wine."

☞Sir Winston Churchill, "We will fight on the land and on the sea and in the air."

UPDATING: "And in the kitchens and in the dental chairs."

☞Shakespeare, "Heavy lies the head that wears a crown."

UPDATING: "Verily, whether the king got it from his kingdom or his dentist."

IRISH PROVERB: "There is nothing like baking soda for making Irish bread."

UPDATING: "Or putting out kitchen fires, or cleaning teeth."

YOU CAN LEARN A LOT FROM
YOUR KIDS ABOUT "FIXEN" EGGS

"Spray some of that Pam stuff on a frying pan. No, not the outside, just the inside part where the eggs are going into. Use the low heat place on the knob thing and open up a can of tomatoes and put them right by the stove. Break a couple of eggs into the pan. Try real hard to keep the shell pieces out of the pan. Stir it all around with a wooden spoon. The wooden spoon doesn't make so much noise and

wake everybody up. Add some pepper and put some of the tomatoes in, and keep stirring while you sing a song like Mommy does. You can turn the eggs over if you can reach the "what'cha call it." Then you scrape them onto a plate and carry them to the bedroom. Give her a hug and say, "I love you, Mommy."

DADDY'S PRAYER FOR HIS KIDS

Lord, help me to get them through pediatrics, orthodontics, and Little League, and fast food places. Help me to say no when I should say no, and tell them I don't know when I really don't know. And, what you could do for me, Lord, is to help me find some more time, because I know the most important thing I can give my kids is time.

Chapter 18

Units of Measure or
Words To Cook By

Cocktail parties are often attended by two kinds of people. The first kind are the sort of people who use words in a way that the second kind of people don't understand. This does not mean in itself that the first kind are snobs and the second are bimbos. No, it usually means that the first kind have been spending so much time in a particular specialized activity that they have slipped into the habit of employing their secret vocational words right out in public.

Riding in a cab to Kennedy Airport in New York City the taxi pulled abreast of another cab at a red light. My driver said to the other cabbie, "What donkeys are you riding tomorrow?" I had visions of the other cabbie being assigned to drive a team of mules pulling an open carriage through Central Park. Fortunately, my driver later explained that he was looking for a tip on tomorrow's horse race.

While I was reclining on a dental couch my dentist said to his assistant, "Give me an explorer and a reverse mallet." I had visions of Gunga Din charging in with a double-headed sledgehammer.

Great cooks are like cab drivers and members of the medical profession, they have developed a specialized meaning for the words they frequently use. These special meaning words can be particularly confusing, and sometimes funny, to the lay person. This is true when the words refer to measurements employed in the preparation

of foodstuff. Listening to my wife take an apple pie through its birthing process can be a mystifying experience with special food measuring terms. She proceeds: " SOME Granny apples, a SLATHER of flour, SOME shortening, a LITTLE water, a couple of PINCHES of sugar and cinnamon; some DABS of butter, a TAD more sugar and we're ready to hit it at 425 for a SPELL and then back off to 350 for a BIT. We'll run a broom straw through the top to see if it's done. No! I know it's done, it SMELLS just right!

HERE IS A WELL ABRIDGED DICTIONARY,

SHOWING HOW MUCH TO USE WHEN THE RECIPE SAYS "SOME" OR—

BIT: Take a look at your sandwich; the amount missing after your first bite.

BITE: The amount the average person can chew at one time; exclude all people who bite off more than they can chew.

BLOB: One "running over" tablespoon or the amount of ketchup that makes a BLOB on a clean floor.

BLUB: First part of **BLUBBER**; used by cooks who speak in one syllable words.

BLUBBER: Since we now understand that it is wrong to get it from whales, we are entirely dependent upon chronic complainers.

BLURB: Gelett Burgiss who coined this word advised against using it in recipes; this word is reserved for media use only, for example, "the blurb about the weather in Alaska."

BROBDINGNAGIAN: A gigantic amount from Jonathan Swift's *Gulliver's Travels* in the land of the giants; always used in Texas recipes and family picnics.

BUNCH: A very small **BROBDINGNAGIAN.**

BURB: 2/3 of a **BURBLE**.

BURBLE: What comes out of an uncorked bottle when you hold it upside down.

BURP: Directly follows eating; if you are embarrassed, say: "Sorry, my shoes are tight!"

DAB: What you get when you wet your finger and stick it in the sugar bowl.

DASH: A BIT less than a **DOLLOP** and a whole lot less than a DRACHMA.

DISCRETE AMOUNT: Sometimes employed in cooking as a warning against too much; sometimes used in clothing as a warning against too little.

DOLLOP: Two or more jiggers.

DRACHM: Old spelling of DRACHMA when only one **A** was allowed per word.

DRACHMA: As much as you can hold in one hand; in ancient Greece the amount required in taxes from each citizen (all qualified tax collectors wore glove size XL).

DRAM: Dry measure, 1/16 of an ounce or 4/1000th of a pound, if you don't do arithmetic use a **PINCH.**

DROP: In the singular form, an impossible amount to get out of a bottle.

FARL: As found in Irish cookbooks: to **FARL** a furl means to roll out the oaten cake dough and cut into four quarters, that is a **FARL,** and bake until the **FARLS,** that is the quarters furl, that is curl.

FLUB: When you have used a **GLUB** instead of a **DAB.**

GENEROUS AMOUNT: Two **TITHES,** or two tenths of all that you have.

GLOB: A very large DROP.

GLUB: See GLUG.

GLUG: Hold uncorked jug on shoulder and make a quick bow. In the Shetland Islands, a dish made with milk and uncooked oatmeal. The first definition tastes better if it's Scotch.

GRIND: As much as you can twist a hand grinding pepper mill without changing your grip.

HANDFUL: See **DRACHMA.**

HUMONGOUS: Two **DRACHMAS** or two **HANDFULS.**

IOTA: What you don't have one of when you are completely out of it.

JOT: Same as IOTA; somewhere in ancient times the **J** and **I** were mixed up and the **A** was forgotten.

JIGGER: 1 1\2 liquid ounces, a good bartender working for the house can get this down to a half ounce.

LARDER: Originally used as a noun to designate the place where the foodstuff was stashed; now used as a verb with the preposition <u>IN</u> following, for example: to make gumbo you have to **LARDER IN** some okra.

LILLIPUTIAN: Little; again from J. Swift's colorful travelogues; in cooking about half as much as you had intended to use.

LOT: As in real estate, could be a little lot or a big lot; try a PASSEL and then taste.

MITE: An amount equal in size to one of those little bugs that gets into the flour sack.

MODICUM: A moderate amount, i.e., half as much as you used last time.

MONDO: See **BROBDINGNAGIAN.**

MOTE: 2 Mites.

NUT SIZE: Vague term used by vague cooks, request clarification, viz, are we talking peanuts or coconuts.

PASSEL: Couple of **BUNCHES.**

PEA SIZE: Always keep one freshly depodded pea in the fridge for handy reference.

PEPPER: To **PEPPER** not necessarily with pepper; about two **SPRINKLES.**

PINCH: In Rome, a despicable or enjoyable habit, depending on whether you are the "pinchee" or the pincher; in the rest of the world, the amount that can be held between the thumb and the forefinger. Don't fret about some people having smaller thumbs. Nature provides for the little ones to require less of whatever they are pinching.

PLETHORA: A great many, an excess; several **BUNCHES.** When you have a **PLETHORA** you always have SOME left over.

SLATHER: As much as necessary to cover whatever is being slathered to a depth of 1/4 inch.

SLEW: Several **BUNCHES**; equivalent to the number of soldiers slain every time the Philistines went out **SLEWING.**

SLUG: Two jiggers, well—maybe three.

SMELL: One of the decision-making sensors used by cooks; example: In buying fresh fish — if it does, it isn't.

SMIDGEN: A small amount added just before tasting, to see if you have already put in too much.

SNUFF: What you say when the cook has put in "nuff" pepper.

SNIP: A unit of measure usually employed with parsley and a pair of scissors.

SOME: A generous **HANDFUL** more or less.

SPECK: A couple of MITES.

SPELL: Unit of time, about the duration of a child's fascination with a new toy.

SPIT: The size of one of the things that is illegal to do in a public place.

SPLASH: One **GLUG** from a gallon jug.

SPOT: What some inhabitants of the United Kingdom order when they want a cup of tea.

SPRINKLE: The amount deposited during one pass of the lawn sprinkler.

SPRINKLING: A **Passel** of **Sprinkles.**

SQUIRT: A cook weighing less than 75 pounds.

SPRITZ: A small **SQUIRT.**

SPRITZER: One who **SPRINKLES** a **SQUIRT.**

TAD: Just the right amount of any ingredient; if in doubt try half a **SMIDGEN.**

TASTE: What every good cook does every two minutes.

TEXAS DIPPER: A water dowser from Dallas.

TEST: A must in all food preparation; to test whether it is a mushroom or a toadstool, eat one. If you "ain't", it wasn't.

TITHE: One tenth of "**SOMETHING**".

TOUCH: Half a DAB.

TURN: Output of a pepper mill per revolution.

WALNUT SIZE: A one inch **BLOB.**

WHIT: Smallest amount possible; used in the negative sense: "Don't use a WHIT of salt."

WHISPER: 2 or 3 TOUCHES; the precise amount of perfume worn by a charming and beautiful woman.

AS A SCIENCE COOKING MAY NOT BE
AS PRECISE AS ASTROPHYSICS
BUT IT REQUIRES MORE ACCURACY
THAN GOVERNMENT ECONOMICS.

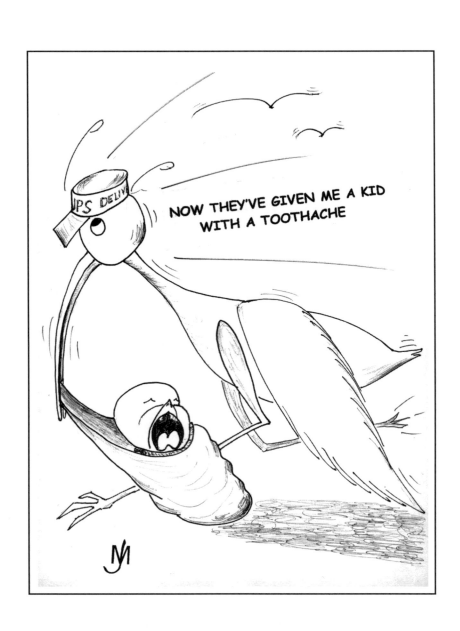

INDEX

ABOUT THE AUTHOR

Jim Moran has devoted over twenty years to the improvement of food quality. From McDonald hamburgers to Hershey candy bars, from Hawaiian sugar to Taiwanese rice, his objective has been to make food better and safer for the consumer. Holder of six U.S., Canadian, and European patents on food inspection systems he was chosen to receive the Outstanding Achievement Award in the field of engineering in 1981 from his alma mater, Rutgers University.

A member and national fellow of the Explorers club with head-quarters in New York City, he has completed special assignments in the remotest regions of the Artic as well as the steaming jungles of New Guinea. He served with the United States scientific delegation in Helsinki, Finland during the International Geophysical Year.

Cuisine Après Dentist

He was formerly a research associate at Harvard University and more recently the CEO of B&D Laboratories, a research and development company based in New England.

A frequent contributor to newspaper Sunday feature articles on food, travel, and science, he has served as lecturer and raconteur for Rotary International and the Food Packaging Institute. As a licensed pilot, he has flown sailplanes, airplanes, and balloons. He is an avid amateur radio operator but first and foremost he loves to cook.

RUTLEDGE BOOKS, INC.
107 Mill Plain Road #302
Danbury, CT 06811

Please send me _____ copies of *Cuisine Après Dentist, All About Cooking, Eating, Laughing, And Helping Yourself After You've Been To The Dentist* @ $12.95 per copy plus $3.50 S&H. Send check or money order or call 1-800-278-8533.

Name: _____

Address: _____

City: _____ State: ___ Zip: _____

Phone Number: _____

Prices subject to change without notice.
Please allow 3-5 weeks for delivery.

RUTLEDGE BOOKS, INC.
107 Mill Plain Road #302
Danbury, CT 06811

Please send me _____ copies of *Cuisine Après Dentist, All About Cooking, Eating, Laughing, And Helping Yourself After You've Been To The Dentist* @ $12.95 per copy plus $3.50 S&H. Send check or money order or call 1-800-278-8533.

Name: _____

Address: _____

City: _____ State: ___ Zip: _____

Phone Number: _____

Prices subject to change without notice.
Please allow 3-5 weeks for delivery.